The Reconstruction of Iraq after 2003

MENA DEVELOPMENT REPORT

The Reconstruction of Iraq after 2003

Learning from Its Successes and Failures

Hideki Matsunaga

© 2019 International Bank for Reconstruction and Development / The World Bank
1818 H Street NW, Washington, DC 20433
Telephone: 202-473-1000; Internet: www.worldbank.org

Some rights reserved
1 2 3 4 22 21 20 19

This work is a product of the staff of The World Bank with external contributions. The findings, interpretations, and conclusions expressed in this work do not necessarily reflect the views of The World Bank, its Board of Executive Directors, or the governments they represent. The World Bank does not guarantee the accuracy of the data included in this work. The boundaries, colors, denominations, and other information shown on any map in this work do not imply any judgment on the part of The World Bank concerning the legal status of any territory or the endorsement or acceptance of such boundaries.

Nothing herein shall constitute or be considered to be a limitation upon or waiver of the privileges and immunities of The World Bank, all of which are specifically reserved.

Rights and Permissions

This work is available under the Creative Commons Attribution 3.0 IGO license (CC BY 3.0 IGO) http://creativecommons.org/licenses/by/3.0/igo. Under the Creative Commons Attribution license, you are free to copy, distribute, transmit, and adapt this work, including for commercial purposes, under the following conditions:

Attribution—Please cite the work as follows: Matsunaga, Hideki. 2019. *The Reconstruction of Iraq after 2003: Learning from Its Successes and Failures.* MENA Development Report Series. Washington, DC: World Bank. doi:10.1596/978-1-4648-1390-0. License: Creative Commons Attribution CC BY 3.0 IGO

Translations—If you create a translation of this work, please add the following disclaimer along with the attribution: *This translation was not created by The World Bank and should not be considered an official World Bank translation. The World Bank shall not be liable for any content or error in this translation.*

Adaptations—If you create an adaptation of this work, please add the following disclaimer along with the attribution: *This is an adaptation of an original work by The World Bank. Views and opinions expressed in the adaptation are the sole responsibility of the author or authors of the adaptation and are not endorsed by The World Bank.*

Third-party content—The World Bank does not necessarily own each component of the content contained within the work. The World Bank therefore does not warrant that the use of any third-party-owned individual component or part contained in the work will not infringe on the rights of those third parties. The risk of claims resulting from such infringement rests solely with you. If you wish to re-use a component of the work, it is your responsibility to determine whether permission is needed for that re-use and to obtain permission from the copyright owner. Examples of components can include, but are not limited to, tables, figures, or images.

All queries on rights and licenses should be addressed to World Bank Publications, The World Bank Group, 1818 H Street NW, Washington, DC 20433, USA; e-mail: pubrights@worldbank.org.

ISBN (paper): 978-1-4648-1390-0
ISBN (electronic): 978-1-4648-1391-7
DOI: 10.1596/978-1-4648-1390-0

Cover photo: © iStock.com/sasacvetkovic33. Used with permission. Further permission required for reuse.
Cover design: Bill Pragluski, Critical Stages LLC

Library of Congress Cataloging-in-Publication Data has been applied for

MENA Development Report Series

This series features major development reports from the Middle East and North Africa region of the World Bank, based on new research and thoroughly peer-reviewed analysis. Each report aims to enrich the debate on the main development challenges and opportunities the region faces as it strives to meet the evolving needs of its people.

Titles in the MENA Development Report Series

The Reconstruction of Iraq after 2003: Learning from Its Successes and Failures (2019) by Hideki Matsunaga

Beyond Scarcity: Water Security in the Middle East and North Africa (2018) by World Bank

Jobs or Privileges: Unleashing the Employment Potential of the Middle East and North Africa (2015) by Marc Schiffbauer, Abdoulaye Sy, Sahar Hussain, Hania Sahnoun, and Philip Keefer

The Road Traveled: Dubai's Journey towards Improving Private Education: A World Bank Review (2014) by Simon Thacker and Ernesto Cuadra

Inclusion and Resilience: The Way Forward for Social Safety Nets in the Middle East and North Africa (2013) by Joana Silva, Victoria Levin, and Matteo Morgandi

Opening Doors: Gender Equality and Development in the Middle East and North Africa (2013) by World Bank

From Political to Economic Awakening in the Arab World: The Path of Economic Integration (2013) by Jean-Pierre Chauffour

Adaptation to a Changing Climate in the Arab Countries: A Case for Adaptation Governance and Leadership in Building Climate Resilience (2012) by Dorte Verner

Renewable Energy Desalination: An Emerging Solution to Close the Water Gap in the Middle East and North Africa (2012) by World Bank

Poor Places, Thriving People: How the Middle East and North Africa Can Rise Above Spatial Disparities (2011) by World Bank

Financial Access and Stability: A Road Map for the Middle East and North Africa (2011) by Roberto R. Rocha, Zsofia Arvai, and Subika Farazi

From Privilege to Competition: Unlocking Private-Led Growth in the Middle East and North Africa (2009) by World Bank

The Road Not Traveled: Education Reform in the Middle East and North Africa (2008) by World Bank

Making the Most of Scarcity: Accountability for Better Water Management Results in the Middle East and North Africa (2007) by World Bank

Gender and Development in the Middle East and North Africa: Women in the Public Sphere (2004) by World Bank

Unlocking the Employment Potential in the Middle East and North Africa: Toward a New Social Contract (2004) by World Bank

Better Governance for Development in the Middle East and North Africa: Enhancing Inclusiveness and Accountability (2003) by World Bank

Trade, Investment, and Development in the Middle East and North Africa: Engaging with the World (2003) by World Bank

All books in the MENA Development Report series are available for free at https://openknowledge.worldbank.org/handle/10986/2168.

Contents

Acknowledgments   xi
Abbreviations   xiii

Overview   1
    The Context for Iraq's Reconstruction   2
    The International Response to Iraq's Reconstruction Needs   4
    Reconstruction's Impact on Iraq's Economy and Job Creation   5
    The Reconstruction of Infrastructure, Human Capital, and
        Social Services   7
    Governance, Institutional Reform, and
        Private Sector Development   9
    Lessons for International Donors and Organizations   10
    Recommendations for Future Reconstruction   16
    Methodology   18
    References   18

1 Reconstruction Challenges in Iraq   19
    Introduction   19
    Security   20
    Institutions   21
    The Economy   24
    Annex 1A: Phases of Iraqi Reconstruction, March 2003
        to June 2014   30
    Notes   33
    References   33

2 International Engagement in the Reconstruction of Iraq   35
    Overview of International Actors   35
    Key Actors in the International Response   38
    Challenges to the International Response   48

Notes	54
References	55

3 The Reconstruction of Iraqi Infrastructure and Human Capital — 57

The Electricity Sector	57
The Oil Sector	63
The Education Sector	67
The Health Sector	71
Notes	74
References	75

4 Institution Building, Governance Reform, and Private Sector Development — 77

Capacity Development and Institution Building	77
Governance Reform: Decentralization and Local Governance	81
Governance Reform: Tackling Corruption	84
Private Sector Development	87
Annex 4A: Disputes over Decentralization in Iraq	90
Notes	91
References	92

5 Lessons Learned from the Reconstruction of Iraq — 95

Working with National Institutions and Cultivating National Ownership	95
Effective Implementation in Insecure Environments	97
Improving the Effectiveness of Donor Funding for Reconstruction	99
Enhancing Accountability in Reconstruction	102
Improving the Assessment Process and Prioritization	104
Donor Coordination with National Institutions	106
Procurement and Contracting	107
Notes	110
References	110

6 Recommendations for Future Reconstruction Operations — 113

Reconstruction in Fragile and Conflict Settings: Uncertain, Fluid, and Complex	113
Reinforcing National Success	114
Balancing Time and Scale in Operations	116
Promoting Private Sector Engagement in Fragile Settings	117

Reinforcing the Security-Development Nexus 118
The Future of Reconstruction in Fragile and Conflict Settings 118
References 119

Boxes

2.1 The Oil-for-Food Programme 47
4.1 Institution Building in Iraq: The Fiscal Management
 Information System 80

Figures

O.1 Documented Civilian Deaths from Violence in Iraq,
 January 2003 to February 2017 3
O.2 Funding Sources for Iraq Reconstruction, 2003–12 5
O.3 GDP per Capita and Crude Oil Prices in Iraq, 1970–2014 6
O.4 Core Public Sector Employment in Iraq, 2003–15 6
O.5 Electricity Generation Capacity in Iraq, 2002–14 7
O.6 Electricity Supply from the National Grid in Iraq,
 2007, 2011, and 2012 8
O.7 Crude Oil Production in Iraq before and after International
 Private Sector Engagement, 2003–15 9
1.1 Civilian Deaths from Violence in the Anbar, Baghdad, Basra,
 and Erbil Governorates of Iraq, 2003–16 21
1.2 Oil Production and Exports in Iraq, 1980–2014 25
1.3 GDP per Capita and Crude Oil Prices in Iraq, 1970–2014 25
1.4 Government Revenue and Oil Price Fluctuations in Iraq,
 2003–15 26
1.5 Investment Budget Execution in Iraq, 2005–13 27
1.6 Core Public Sector Employment in Iraq, 2003–15 29
1.7 Average Composition of Public Expenditures in Iraq, 2005–10 29
1A.1 Oil Production, Electricity Generation, and Iraqi Investment
 Expenditures, 2002–13 32
2.1 Pledges Made at the International Donor Conference for
 Iraq Reconstruction, October 2003 36
2.2 Funding Sources for Iraq Reconstruction, 2003–12 37
2.3 Allocation of the U.K. Budget for Iraq's Reconstruction,
 2003–July 2004 42
2.4 Annual European Union Commitment for Development and
 Humanitarian Assistance to Iraq, 2003–13 43
2.5 Allocation of Japanese Grant Assistance to Iraq, 2003–09 43
2.6 Japanese Loan Assistance to Iraq, 2006–13 44
2.7 Donor Coordination Mechanism Led by Iraqi Entities 49
3.1 Electricity Generation Capacity in Iraq, 2002–14 58

3.2	Electricity Generation in Iraq, Average for May 2003 to December 2005	59
3.3	Electricity Supply from the National Grid in Iraq, 2007, 2011, and 2012	62
3.4	Public Perceptions of Electricity Service Provision in Iraq, by Governorate, 2011	63
3.5	Monthly Oil Production in Iraq, 2003–05	64
3.6	Crude Oil Production in Iraq before and after International Oil Company Engagement, 2003–15	66
3.7	Student Enrollment in Iraq, 2005–13	70
3.8	Infant Mortality Rate versus Life Expectancy at Birth in the Middle East and North Africa, 1980 and 2001	72
3.9	Health Expenditures per Capita in Iraq, 2003–14	73
3.10	Public Perceptions of Health Care Services in Iraq, by Region, 2011	74
5.1	Budget Execution in Iraq, 2005–13	100
5.2	The Dual Accountability Dilemma	102
5.3	Estimated Breakdown of U.S. Reconstruction Contracts in Iraq	109

Tables

1.1	Public Perceptions of the Problems Facing Iraq, February 2004	28
2.1	Total Donor Contributions to the International Reconstruction Fund Facility for Iraq (IRFFI)	36
2.2	U.S. Budget Appropriations for Iraq Reconstruction Efforts	38
2.3	Security and the Rule of Law, Cumulative U.S. Obligations as of September 30, 2012	39
3.1	U.S. Budget Allocations for the Iraqi Oil Sector, as of September 30, 2006	65
3.2	Contracts Awarded by Federal Authorities for Hydrocarbon Exploration and Development in Iraq	67
3.3	Types of Expenditures in the Education Budget in Iraq, 2005–11	69
3.4	Structure and Organization of Education in Iraq	71
4.1	Major U.S. Agency for International Development Programs for the Economy and Governance in Iraq, 2003–12	78
4.2	U.S. Agency for International Development Programs for National and Local Governance and Capacity Development in Iraq	82

Acknowledgments

This report was developed and managed by a team led by Hideki Matsunaga and comprised of Riad Houry and Natsuko Yukawa. Thamir Al Ghadhban and Joseph Saba served as external advisors to the team, and Shantayanan Devarajan provided valuable advice and guidance from the beginning of the research until the final draft. Hafez Ghanem and Saroj Kumar Jha chaired review meetings and helped us to consolidate diverse and valuable comments and to finalize the report. Neil O'Reilly provided substantial input and guidance on multiple versions of the draft. The report benefited at various stages from the guidance and comments of World Bank management and staff, including Asad Alam, Abdallah Al Dardari, Nazaneen Ismail Ali, Zainab A Allawi, Rabah Arezki, Raja Rehan Arshad, Lemya Izzet Ayub, Daniel Kiernan Balke, Ferid Belhaj, Franck Bousquet, Kevin Carey, Emmanuel F. Cuvillier, Ibrahim Dajani, Miguel Angel De Corral Martin, Thomas Djurhuus, Faizaa Fatima, Sepehr Fotovat, Abderrahim Fraiji, Katsumasa Hamaguchi, Ellen Hamilton, Syed Mehdi Hassan, Elena Ianchovichina, Robert Bou Jaoude, Omer Karasapan, Claire Khoury, Andrew C. Kircher, Sibel Kulaksiz, Daniel Lederman, Roland Lomme, Pilar Maisterra, Stephan Massing, Piers Merrick, Janet Lynn Minatelli, Nafie Mohammed Mofid, Richard Olowo, Zeinab Partow, Nadia Fernanda Piffaretti, Francesca Recanatini, Yara Salem, Sajjad Ali Shah Sayed, Simon Stolp, Mio Takada, and Kanae Watanabe.

The team also acknowledges the valuable insights offered by experts from Iraq, academia, civil society, international organizations, and donor organizations, including Bisrat Aklilu, Huda Malik Alani, Sherazade Boualia, Derick Brinkerhoff, Arthur Brown, Carel de Rooy, Lukman Faily, Charles Freeman, Matthew Fuller, Gerard Gomez, Shigeru Handa, Naofumi Hashimoto, Fumio Iwai, Bruce Jones, Izuru Kimura, Bruno Lemarquis, Humam Misconi, Kansuke Nagaoka, Haydar Nasser, Shohei Nishimura, Tomofumi Nishinaga, Haitham Hadi Numan,

Yukio Okamoto, Robin Raphel, Ema Sky, Katsuhiko Takahashi, Jiro Tominaga, Sota Tosaka, Masamichi Toyooka, Kazuto Tsuji, Gary Vogler, Karim Waheed, Tamara Wittes, Fareed Yaseen, and Peter Young.

The team also wishes to acknowledge the tireless support of the World Bank publications team: Susan Graham, Orlando T. Mota, and Jewel McFadden.

Abbreviations

CERP	Commander's Emergency Response Program
COI	Commission of Integrity
CPA	Coalition Provisional Authority
DFI	Development Fund for Iraq
EU	European Union
FMIS	fiscal management information system
IMF	International Monetary Fund
IRFFI	International Reconstruction Fund Facility for Iraq
ISCI	Islamic Supreme Council of Iraq
ISRB	Iraq Strategic Review Board
JICA	Japan International Cooperation Agency
KRG	Kurdistan Regional Government
NGO	nongovernmental organization
OFFP	Oil-for-Food Programme
ORHA	Office of Reconstruction and Humanitarian Assistance
PMAC	Prime Minister's Advisory Commission
PMO	Project Management Office
SIGIR	Special Inspector General for Iraq Reconstruction
SOE	state-owned enterprise
UNDG	United Nations Development Group
UNDGITF	United Nations Development Group Iraq Trust Fund
UNDP	United Nations Development Programme
UNESCO	United Nations Educational, Scientific, and Cultural Organization
UNICEF	United Nations Children's Fund
UNSC	United Nations Security Council
USAID	U.S. Agency for International Development
USACE	U.S. Army Corps of Engineers
WBITF	World Bank Iraq Trust Fund
WHO	World Health Organization

In this study, 1 billion = 1,000 million.

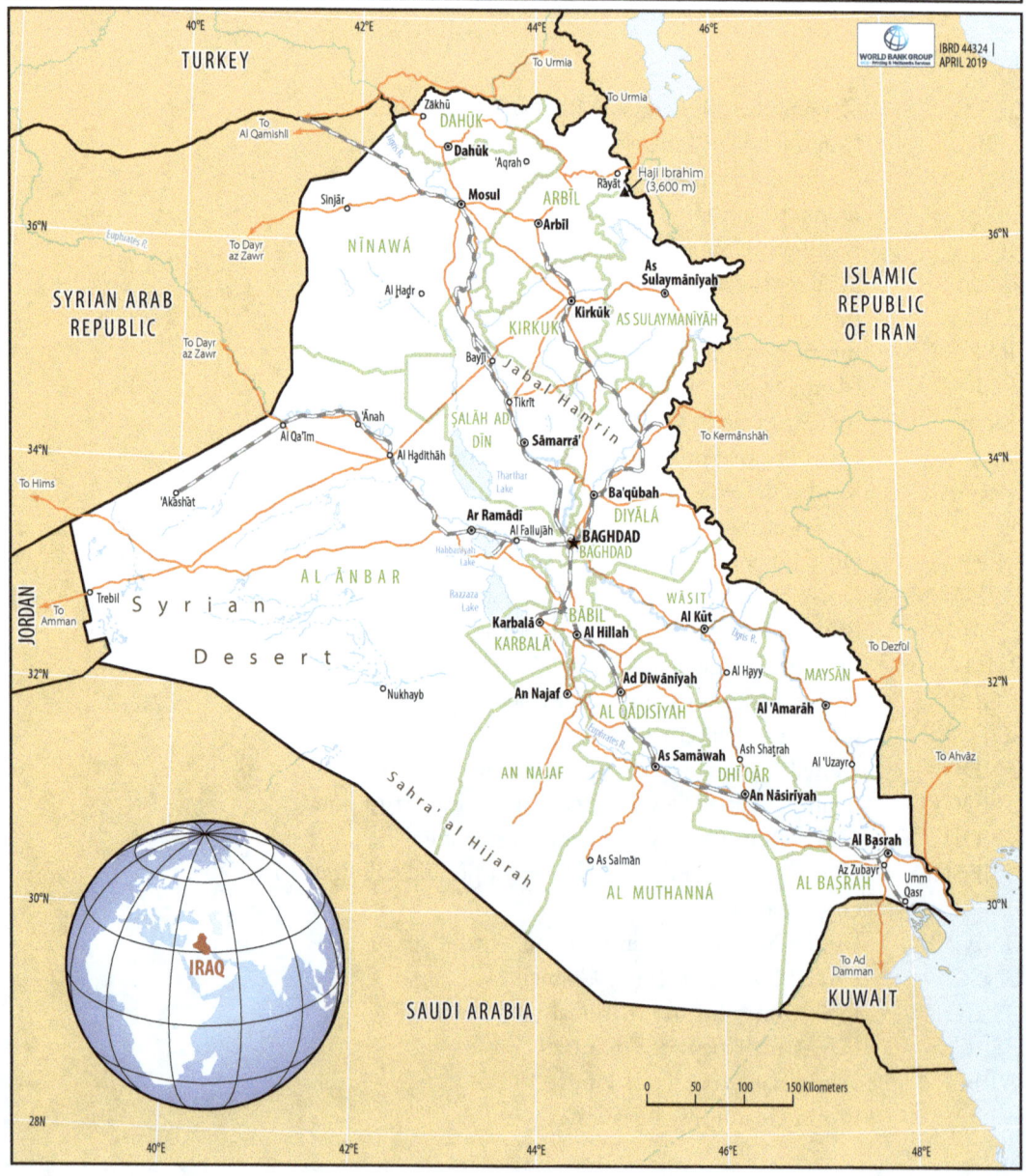

Overview

Pursuing effective reconstruction within contexts of conflict and fragility is a formidable challenge, subject as it is to an uncertain, fluid, and complex environment. Conditions on the ground are dynamic and nonlinear; political, economic, security, and social dynamics are always changing. Amid such difficulties, the international community may hesitate to engage in robust reconstruction activities, but the cost of inaction can be great. The success or failure of country-level reconstruction efforts can have a significant impact on the peace and stability of the broader global community. So how can we manage the process effectively?

In order to find a more effective approach for reconstruction in conflict and fragile settings, we need to learn from past reconstruction experiences. To this end, the reconstruction of Iraq after 2003 offers many lessons. Between 2003 and 2014, more than US$220 billion was spent on reconstruction efforts following the United States–led invasion and overthrow of the Saddam Hussein regime. Despite the huge amount of money spent and the implementation of extensive projects and programs, the international community and the Iraqi people largely view the reconstruction of Iraq in a negative light. Through the course of this research, many interviewees from various government agencies involved in the process said that the impact of reconstruction remains disappointingly obscure considering the resources committed. More recently, after years of fighting the Islamic State of Iraq and the Levant (ISIL), also known as Daesh, the international community and the Iraqi government need to begin planning for a new wave of reconstruction in which the same mistakes are not repeated. The Iraqi reconstruction experience after 2003 offers few successes and many failures from which the international community can learn.

This study seeks to draw out those lessons and to provide recommendations for future reconstruction activities by examining the reconstruction process from 2003 until May 2014, before the emergence of Daesh. The question of what went wrong in Iraq has been the topic of many books, articles, and academic papers. Most analyses address U.S. policies, military intervention, and Iraqi politics, while reviews of the reconstruction process are often limited to each donor's operation. This research reviews the reconstruction of Iraq more broadly.

To draw lessons, the study assesses several dimensions of Iraq's reconstruction. First, it considers the response of key international actors, such as the United Nations (UN), the World Bank, the United States and other bilateral donors—specifically, the European Union, Japan, and the United Kingdom—as well as nongovernmental organizations (NGOs). Second, it analyzes the process and results of the reconstruction of key sectors—electricity, oil, education, and health—in addition to interventions pertaining to institution building and governance reform, with a focus on decentralization, corruption, and private sector development. This study also touches on issues that merit further elaboration in future research, including the responses of international actors to humanitarian and security needs and broader governance and social issues, such as poverty, gender, and youth.

The Context for Iraq's Reconstruction

The conduct of reconstruction in fragile settings is made so difficult because such a wide range of factors impinge on it. In postconflict or inconflict operations, economic, political, security, and social conditions are subject to significant change and regional variance. Iraq was no different, but unlike some postconflict cases, the reconstruction of Iraq was not concerned merely with ensuring economic recovery to the preconflict levels of 2003. Damage from military operations during the invasion itself was limited; rather, the deterioration of infrastructure as well as institutions had been well under way long before the invasion. Stakeholders faced several other critical challenges to their operations.

First, a lack of security presented the most serious challenge for reconstruction activities. During the height of violence in 2006 and 2007, there were as many as 100 civilian deaths per day. As of February 2017—almost 14 years after the invasion—it is estimated that total Iraqi civilian deaths numbered more than 180,000 (figure O.1). Many Iraqi officials who were engaged in reconstruction activities were among the dead. Violence affected foreign aid workers and contractors too. With worsening security and lingering ambiguity over their status and mandate, the UN and many international organizations chose to evacuate staff from Iraq by the end of 2003. For several years, most donors conducted many of their reconstruction operations from outside the country. During that period, the United Kingdom and the United States each kept a large

FIGURE O.1

Documented Civilian Deaths from Violence in Iraq, January 2003 to February 2017

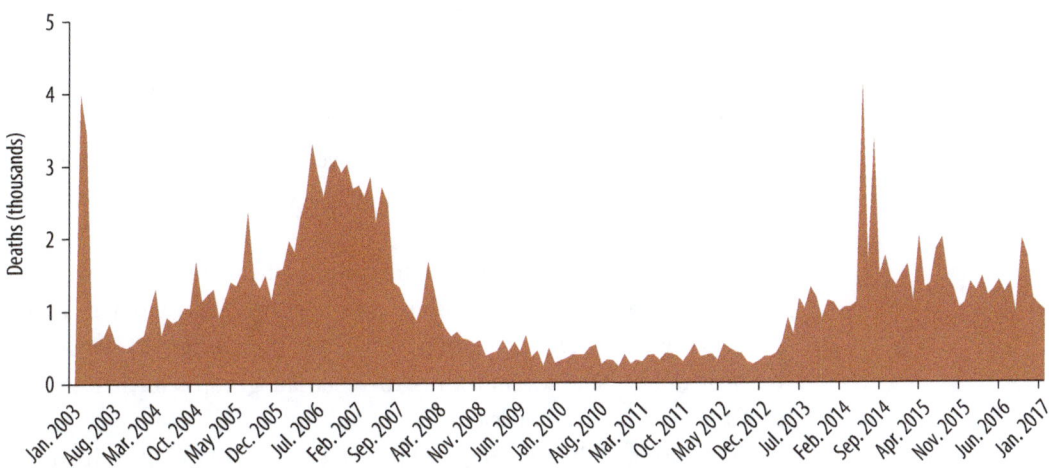

Source: Iraq Body Count data (https://www.iraqbodycount.org/).

presence inside Iraq and continued their reconstruction efforts, although mobility within the country was highly constrained. The need for added security increased the cost of all activities and precluded many others that would have been undertaken in a less volatile postconflict environment. Iraq represents an example of in-conflict reconstruction rather than postconflict reconstruction.

Second, reconstruction activities began when the capacity, roles, and functions of the state and institutions were weak and contested, often violently. In any fragile and conflict-affected situation, weak institutional capacity is a hindrance to reconstruction activities. Considered among the most capable countries in the region during the 1970s and early 1980s, Iraq's institutional capacity was significantly degraded by 2003 following decades of war and economic sanctions. After the invasion in 2003, the occupation force assumed direct responsibility for governing the country in lieu of a national government. Even after sovereignty was returned to Iraq in June 2004, the government's status remained interim and transitional. The weakened role and function of the state, coupled with eroded institutional capacity and practical difficulties in performing the basic tasks of governance, made enhancing government legitimacy through successful reconstruction very difficult.

Third, intensifying ethnosectarian divisions commanded influence over ministries and institutions, severely hampering their effective functioning. Ethnosectarian divisions among Iraqis existed well before the invasion in 2003. The Kurds in the north were long marginalized and oppressed by the Saddam regime, while a Shia uprising against the ruling Saddam regime took place after the Gulf War in 1991. Despite these tensions, ethnosectarian divisions prior to 2003 paled in comparison with the deadly nature of the divisions that followed. Indeed, prior to the invasion, ethnosectarian differences had only limited influence on the Iraqi government and its institutions, partly because they were less consequential under the oppression of the Saddam regime. After the invasion and the regime's collapse, however, groups began emphasizing their differences to enhance their political leverage, further intensifying divisions within the country.

Fourth, external actors competing for influence intensified Iraqi divisions and exacerbated institutional dysfunction. International actors, particularly neighboring countries, frequently intervened in Iraqi politics by providing resources and arms to sectarian groups, further stoking sectarian and political divisions.

Fifth, although Iraq has huge oil resources—some 115 billion barrels of known reserves, the world's fifth largest—and significant gas reserves, the country's existing and potential wealth has presented many challenges that state institutions have yet to overcome. The Iraqi economy's reliance on oil revenues makes it highly vulnerable to oil price fluctuations. In addition, given that the oil sector is highly capital intensive, it has a limited impact on employment generation, and the high resource concentration in the sector has constrained the development of non-oil sectors. Meanwhile, the uneven geographic distribution of oil resources has fueled regional and sectarian disputes, and continuing security and political uncertainty has constrained the modernization and expansion of Iraq's oil and natural gas potential. These challenges are typical consequences of a "resource curse."

The International Response to Iraq's Reconstruction Needs

Beginning in 2003, diverse and significant actors, both domestic and international, engaged in reconstruction activities in Iraq, and the total budget committed to Iraq's reconstruction was unprecedented among postconflict operations undertaken by the international community. At the Madrid Donor Conference in October 2003, the international community—represented by 38 countries, the European Commission, the International Monetary Fund, and the World Bank—announced overall and indicative pledges amounting to more than US$33 billion in grants and loans. These initial commitments expanded significantly over the course of reconstruction. For example, while the United States pledged US$18.6 billion at the conference, the largest donor pledge, U.S. commitments had grown to US$60 billion by the end of 2012. As Iraqi oil production and exports

FIGURE O.2

Funding Sources for Iraq Reconstruction, 2003–12

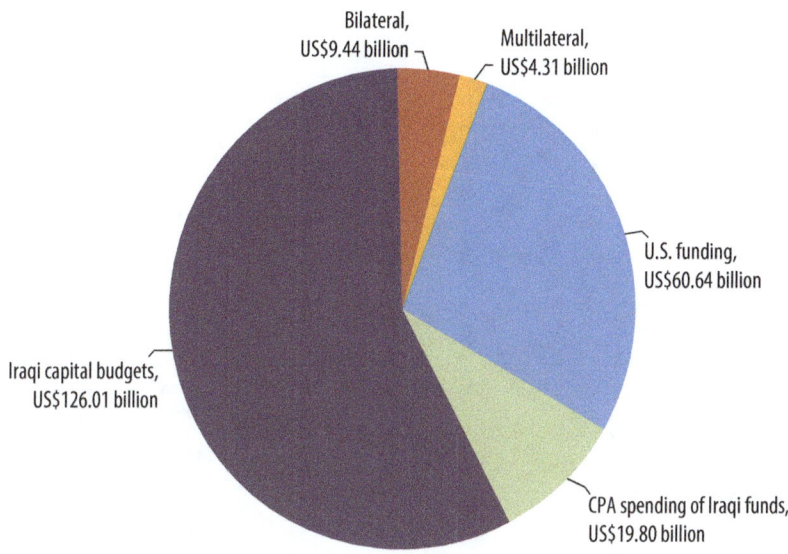

Source: SIGIR 2013.
Note: Total = US$220 billion. CPA = Coalition Provisional Authority.

began to recover, a substantial amount of capital investment was allocated to reconstruction activities. As shown in figure O.2, funding for reconstruction activities came from diverse sources, the largest of which was the Iraqi capital budget, followed by U.S. assistance. The total financial commitment for the reconstruction of Iraq amounted to US$220.1 billion.

Reconstruction's Impact on Iraq's Economy and Job Creation

As far as reconstruction's impact on the economy is concerned, the most critical shortcoming was that reconstruction failed to diversify the Iraqi economy away from its dependence on oil revenues and made little headway in developing the non-oil private sector. Thus, employment in the productive sectors has lagged, while incomes and service delivery remain highly vulnerable to fluctuations in oil prices (figure O.3). While the capital-intensive oil sector employs only 1–2 percent of Iraq's labor force, oil revenues provide the government with abundant resources to generate employment opportunities. By 2008, 40 percent of the Iraqi labor force was employed by the public sector (figure O.4). Spending on the salaries of public employees has placed a heavy burden on the fiscal system, constituting more than 30 percent of government spending.

FIGURE O.3

GDP per Capita and Crude Oil Prices in Iraq, 1970–2014

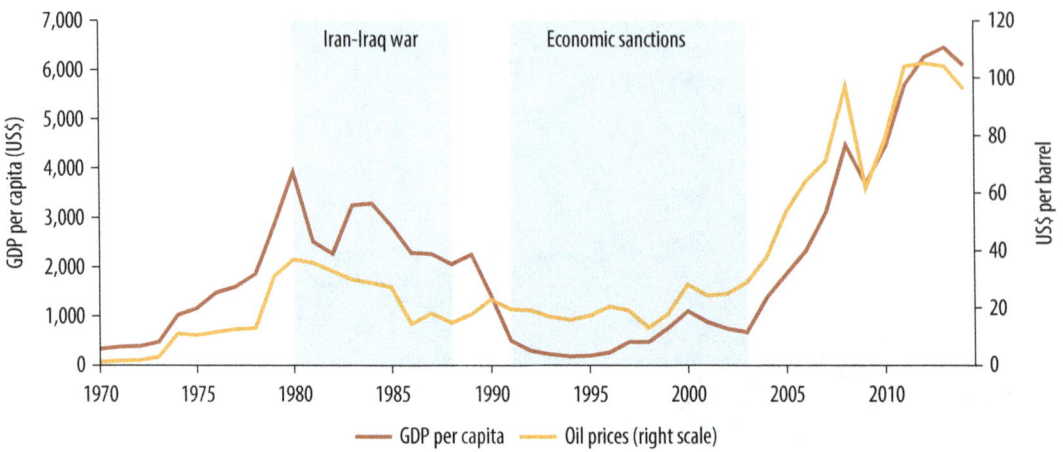

Sources: Economist Intelligence Unit data; World Bank data.

FIGURE O.4

Core Public Sector Employment in Iraq, 2003–15

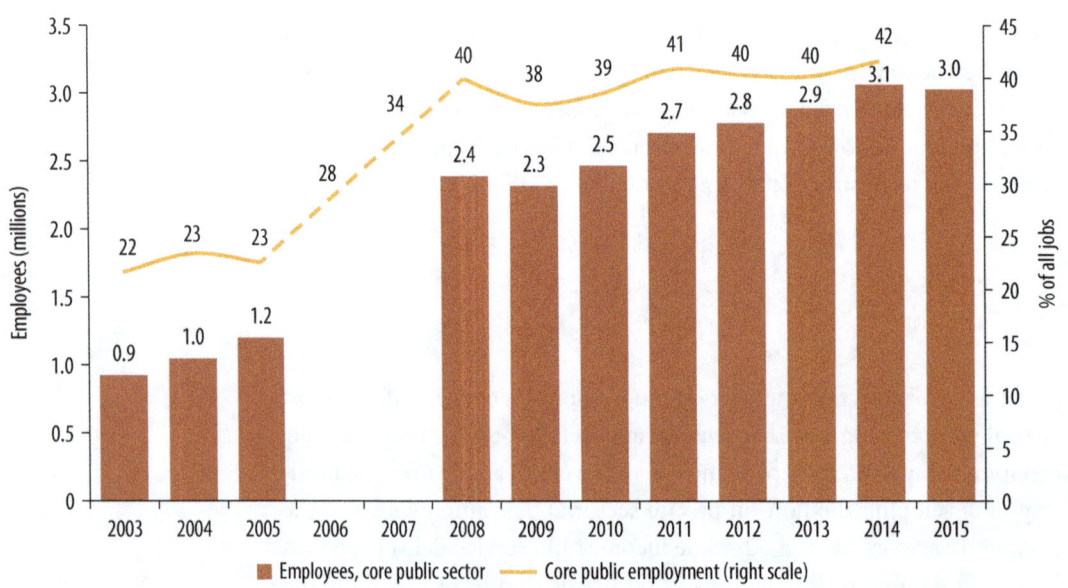

Sources: Iraq Ministry of Finance data; World Development Indicators data from World Bank 2017.

Because of an inflexible budget system, nonsalary spending—in particular, the capital investment budget for reconstruction—had to be cut back when oil prices fell after 2014. Economic diversification and job creation in the non-oil private sector have remained stagnant and continue to be key challenges for the Iraqi economy.

The Reconstruction of Infrastructure, Human Capital, and Social Services

Reconstruction brought some improvements to Iraqi livelihoods, but overall progress on service delivery was gradual and limited. This study considers the development of several key sectors after 2003—including those for electricity, oil, education, and health—to assess the impact of donor assistance on service delivery. Despite the billions of dollars spent on reconstruction, sectoral recovery has been slow and limited. For example, electricity generation capacity took almost eight years to reach the original target of 6,000 megawatts set by the Coalition Provisional Authority (CPA) and first projected for mid-2004, which resulted in chronic electricity shortages that left many Iraqis with only a few hours of electricity per day (figures O.5 and O.6).

In addition, for all four sectors assessed, regional disparities in the progress of reconstruction were wide, with northern and southern Iraq following very different trajectories than the central-western part of the country. In general, improvements in the Kurdistan region have been most substantial.

Considering the oil sector to be a high priority because of its capacity to generate resources for reconstruction activities, the United States assigned experienced advisers to the sector to a degree not seen in other areas of the economy, where many inexperienced officials struggled to make an impact. And although the Iraq Ministry of Oil had suffered from a significant brain drain since the early 1990s and the more recent de-Baathification order

FIGURE O.5

Electricity Generation Capacity in Iraq, 2002–14

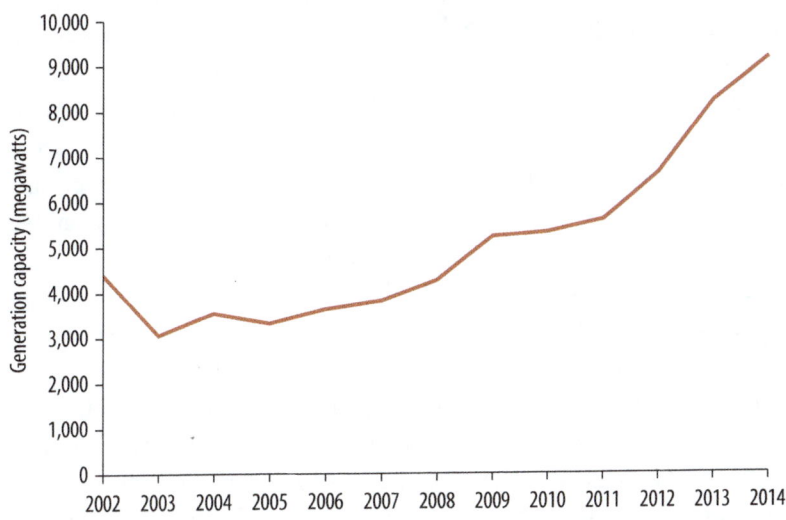

Source: Iraq Ministry of Electricity data.

FIGURE O.6

Electricity Supply from the National Grid in Iraq, 2007, 2011, and 2012

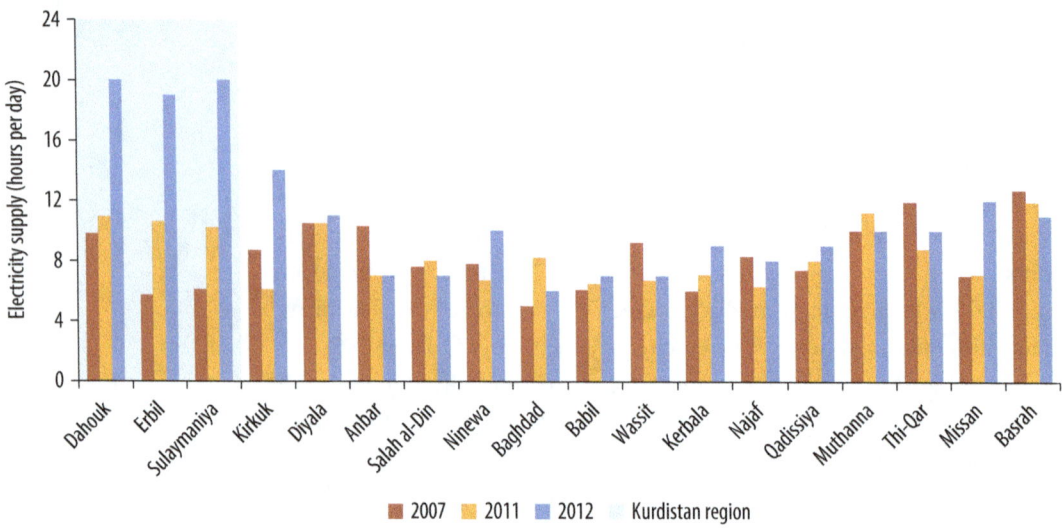

Sources: CSO, KRSO, and United Nations 2011; CSO, KRSO, and World Bank 2007, 2011.

that barred Baathists from senior government roles, it still retained capable management and staff. Nevertheless, like the electricity sector, the oil sector took a long time to reach production and export target levels.

Crude oil production finally began showing strong growth after the oil fields developed by international oil companies went into production in 2010, and increasing Iraqi institutional involvement in the sector's development, along with private sector participation, laid the foundations for further recovery (figure O.7).

During the 1970s and 1980s, Iraq had one of the best education systems in the Middle East and North Africa region. However, years of war and economic sanctions in the 1990s had severely damaged the system by the start of the Iraq War. After 2003, the Iraqi government, with support from donors and international organizations, made a concerted effort to rebuild the country's education system. While they achieved some success on indicators such as enrollment rates in primary school and number of schools built, the quality of education continued to suffer.

Like other sectors, the Iraqi health sector had deteriorated significantly in the decades prior to 2003. Since then, the Iraqi government, donors, and international organizations have committed large resources and energy to restoring the health system, leading to a gradual increase in per capita expenditures in the sector. However, the recovery has been slow, and, although some health indicators have improved, changes have been modest. In particular, this sector has suffered from a large outflow of qualified workers leaving the country.

FIGURE O.7

Crude Oil Production in Iraq before and after International Private Sector Engagement, 2003–15

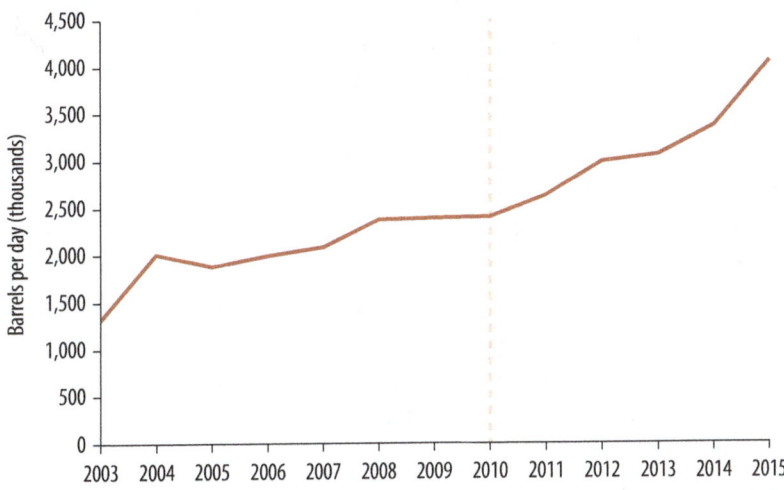

Source: U.S. Energy Information Administration data.

Governance, Institutional Reform, and Private Sector Development

This study focuses on three critical governance issues facing Iraq during the reconstruction period: institutional capacity, decentralization, and corruption. It also assesses donor efforts to foster private sector development. Weak institutional capacity proved to be a major hindrance to the reconstruction process. The deterioration of institutions during the 1980s and 1990s led to a massive brain drain and an erosion in education levels among the Iraqi workforce. Furthermore, actions taken by the CPA after 2003 damaged institutional capacity even further. From the outset, the CPA clearly tended to circumvent existing ministries, public agencies, and Iraqi officials who could have played a bigger role in reconstruction. In addition, the policy of de-Baathification deprived public institutions of some of their existing capacity. To fill the institutional capacity gap, the occupation force brought in many Iraqi exiles from outside of the country, creating tensions with those officials who had remained in Iraq under Saddam. Donors provided numerous training and institution-building programs, but weak institutional capacity continued to hinder reconstruction activities.

Decentralization has been a major preoccupation of postwar Iraqi governance agendas. Prior to 2003, the Iraqi government sat in the middle of a highly centralized system; after the Iraq War, the United States spent more than US$1 billion to promote decentralization as one means of protecting against a reversion to dictatorship. Despite these efforts, as well as the introduction of the new Iraqi Constitution stipulating a federal political system that includes national and local governments, little progress has been made. Disagreements concerning several critical issues have hampered progress, primarily oil revenue–sharing arrangements, the role of the national military and regional and sectarian security forces, and the autonomy of the Kurdistan Regional Government (KRG).

Widespread and intensifying corruption has hampered the reconstruction process. Corruption was rife before the Iraq War, but Saddam's inner circle monopolized the benefits of graft. The war and subsequent pockets of lawlessness, as well as huge inflows of money, exacerbated the degree and extent of corruption. Despite anticorruption initiatives undertaken by the Iraqi government, the United States, and international organizations, corruption remains prevalent, posing a critical challenge for effective governance in Iraq.

Significant efforts were made to develop the private sector, but they failed to diversify the Iraqi economy. Despite large-scale assistance from the United States, UN agencies, and the World Bank, the centrally controlled, oil-dependent economy continued to prevail, creating few job opportunities in the non-oil private sector. The biggest risk factors for foreign and local private actors seeking to invest and expand business activities included the dire security situation, political uncertainty, and the lack of effective mechanisms for lowering risk.

Lessons for International Donors and Organizations

Based on the analysis of international reconstruction efforts and the assessment of their impact on sectors, governance, and institutions, this study identifies lessons for international donors and organizations in seven areas.

Working with National Institutions and Cultivating National Ownership

A critical lesson that the Iraq reconstruction experience reemphasized is that national institutions matter a great deal for the impact and sustainability of reconstruction efforts. In addition:

- International actors need to avoid weakening national institutions and social capital through their interventions. In Iraq, policies such as de-Baathification, dissolution of the Iraqi military, and establishment of the Governing Council based on ethnosectarian divisions have had a lasting negative impact on institutions and society.

- The drive for early results does not justify bypassing national institutions; donors should work through them. A U.S. audit report states that physical infrastructure put in place in Iraq by United States–funded reconstruction was already breaking down by 2005 since Iraqi institutions were not fully engaged, and the roles of institutions in operating and maintaining infrastructure were not sufficiently considered.

- Developing the capacity of national institutions is key for successful reconstruction, but capacity cannot be developed through the provision of training opportunities alone, and donors and international organizations need to review their approaches to capacity development and make them more effective. In Iraq, donors and international organizations provided numerous capacity development programs and training opportunities, but the impact of these assistance programs is unclear. Too often, they were driven by supply and the need to spend reconstruction funds heavily and quickly.

- The international community should reinforce indigenous policies and systems, not impose them. In Iraq, the United States–led occupation force attempted the latter, but its efforts failed because it had given insufficient consideration to the local context.

- Interventions can affect the behavior of national actors in unforeseen ways. In Iraq, as political and sectarian tensions rose, Iraqi officials became increasingly reluctant to make decisions for fear of being accused of engaging in corruption or of favoring one side or the other. International actors need to consider how their own activities can help to cultivate forward-facing behaviors among country partners.

Enhancing Implementation in an Insecure Environment

In a dangerous security environment, how should donors and international organizations respond? There is no one right answer, as the circumstances of organizations and conflicts differ. However, the experience in Iraq offers insights into how organizations might approach future operations under such conditions. For example:

- For effective implementation, it is important for external actors to adopt a bottom-up and flexible approach to deal with the uncertain, fluid, and complex nature of reconstruction. In Iraq, there were serious gaps between the reality of needs and constraints on the ground and what reconstruction projects and programs were trying to achieve.

- Improving the effectiveness of remote management needs further consideration within the specific contexts of affected countries. Due to deteriorating security, post-2003 Iraq became the largest-ever case of remote management of reconstruction operations for the international community, bringing with it many challenges.

- Maintaining a presence within a country under volatile security conditions is extremely challenging and increases the risks for concerned organizations, but it also provides better opportunities to interact with counterparts and enhance the effectiveness of assistance. Retaining a presence in the less volatile parts of a country might allow for more flexible responses to challenges. In the case of Iraq, most donors and international organizations responded inflexibly to the fluctuations of and wide regional differences in the security environment.

- Donors and international organizations need to seize opportunities to effect changes during critical moments—the "golden hours" that can follow immediately after the cessation of fierce fighting. In Iraq, there was some success at this in Basra after a military confrontation in 2008, which resulted in significant improvements in the city's security.

- Efforts should be made to find an effective way for development and security actors to work together to achieve peace and stability from the outset. In Iraq, due to the contentious nature of the invasion and the outsized influence and role of the United States in the first year of reconstruction, systematic communication between development and security actors was limited. Actions in development and security were undertaken independently in a fragmented manner, a problem that improved only moderately with the United States–led military surge in 2007.

Improving the Effectiveness of Donor Funding for Reconstruction

In Iraq, donor funds were provided through bilateral aid, international organizations, or a trust fund, namely, the International Reconstruction Fund Facility for Iraq (IRFFI). But the role of donor funding is not limited to filling a financial gap, and the experience in Iraq offers several lessons concerning how donors provide resources. For example:

- Donors, executing international organizations, and national institutions need to implement reconstruction projects beyond the trust fund framework, giving careful consideration to their impact on the budget and economy of the country in need. While the IRFFI played a role in reconstruction efforts, stakeholders often focused solely on the implementation of specific projects and programs funded by the IRFFI to the exclusion of—and thus limiting the fund's impact on—the Iraqi economy. The execution rate of the Iraqi capital investment budget remained at between 40 percent and 60 percent of spending between 2005 and 2013, while donor funding was poorly coordinated with capital investment projects paid for by the government.

- Information on donor funding needs to be shared with national counterparts. In Iraq, donor funding remained mostly off-budget, so actual project financing was largely opaque to the Iraqi government, which did little to enhance project ownership among Iraqi institutions.

- Donor funding mechanisms should be leveraged to mobilize private resources and to stimulate private sector activities. In Iraq, job creation and long-term growth outside of the oil sector remained limited partly due to the failure to mobilize private funding for the non-oil sector.

Enhancing Accountability in Reconstruction

Diverse issues related to accountability affected the impact of reconstruction in various ways. For example:

- Dual accountability—the tendency among donors and international organizations to be accountable first to their domestic constituencies and stakeholders and only second to those of recipient states—can make delivering results on the ground difficult. In Iraq, superiors back in capitals often overlooked or dismissed the good intentions of international staff in the field.

- When financing for reconstruction comes from external partners, it may not foster domestic accountability since citizens feel less obligated to monitor spending for which they have not paid. External actors should try harder to leverage reconstruction funds to strengthen accountability between national institutions and citizens. The majority of the Iraqi reconstruction budget was funded by oil revenues and donor funding, giving Iraqis little incentive to scrutinize reconstruction spending consistently.

- Poorly managed donor spending on reconstruction can exacerbate existing problems regarding accountability. An effective monitoring mechanism can be achieved by employing new technologies, engaging third parties, and involving multiple national parties. Insufficient monitoring of reconstruction efforts in Iraq resulted not only in the failure of numerous projects and programs, but also in widespread fraud and corruption.

Improving Processes for Needs Assessment and Prioritization

In conflict-affected regions, effective needs assessment faces many challenges beyond safety and security. For example:

- Postconflict reconstruction usually starts with a needs assessment, but the process is often far less effective than it could be. While the joint needs assessment in Iraq helped donors and the international community to understand the basic situation on the ground during the initial stage of reconstruction, it made little use of resources that existed inside Iraq prior to the invasion, it failed to assess institutional capacity, and it lacked a systematic follow-up mechanism.

- In a postconflict environment, assessing citizen needs is invariably difficult, making it all the more important for donors and executing agencies to diversify their network of national counterparts and other information sources as well as their exposure to every part of the country to foster an inclusive, "whole-of-country" approach. In Iraq, most donors had their operational base in the highly fortified International Zone of Baghdad, which restricted their interactions with actors outside of it.

- International actors need to take a more strategic approach to prioritizing the areas of intervention. A lack of security and volatile political conditions constrained donor interactions with Iraqi counterparts, leading to many projects being selected opportunistically.

- Donors and international organizations should not overburden national counterparts with excessive assessment and reporting requirements. The lack of security in Iraq limited donor activities within the country; as a result, donors and international organizations engaged in a vast number of activities that did not require a field presence, such as assessments and analytical reporting and strategy work, most of which—along with the financial resources that funded them—have been of little use since the beginning.

Donor Coordination with National Institutions

Since multiple donors and other stakeholders are often engaged in reconstruction activities, the establishment of an effective coordination mechanism is critical. Some major lessons were learned in Iraq in this regard. For example:

- Careful attention needs to be given to the costs of coordination among donors, and priority should be given to interaction with national counterparts. Since the reconstruction of Iraq took place under extraordinary circumstances, in which most donors were located outside of the country, donors tended to spend most of their time meeting each other and focusing on coordinating between and within agencies rather than interacting with their Iraqi counterparts.

- Better donor coordination can lessen the burden on national institutions. In Iraq, various donors undertook an excessive number of projects with little coordination with each other, causing significant confusion among officials and fragmentation of activities.

- Effective coordination can make capacity development programs more effective. A common problem raised in interviews with former Iraqi officials for this research was the lack of coordination on the substance and approach of capacity development programs.

Procurement and Contracting

Having effective and transparent but flexible, simplified, and swift procurement and contracting processes is critical for project implementation in postconflict settings, as is the need to identify and mitigate the risk of fraud and corruption so as to build trust. In addition:

- With so many active donors, there is a need to harmonize systems and requirements as much as possible to avoid overwhelming the state's capacity. In Iraq, the use of different procurement rules among various donors created significant confusion for Iraqi institutions and officials.

- A flexible application of procurement rules and procedures is critical for implementing reconstruction projects swiftly and effectively. Procurement procedures that were developed for operations in more stable environments were ill-suited to Iraq and hampered the activities of most donors.

- Contract modalities need to be structured carefully to weigh both cost-effectiveness and potential cost increases in unstable environments. Due to the prolonged violence in Iraq, all donors faced spiraling contract prices, as indirect costs, such as those relating to security, grew.

- Interventions relating to repairs, rehabilitation, and new construction need to be weighed carefully. In Iraq, rehabilitation often proved more difficult than greenfield construction.

Recommendations for Future Reconstruction

Since contemporary reconstruction has to be undertaken in volatile situations, there are some instructive analogies between the nature of war and that of reconstruction. Carl von Clausewitz described the countless factors that impinge on the conduct of war as friction (von Clausewitz [1832] 1976). This idea of friction can be applied to reconstruction activities. Friction can be self-induced, caused by mismanagement of the donor process and a lack of coordination of stakeholders, for example. Friction can also be external, such as an unstable security environment threatened by terrorist organizations. Friction in reconstruction can result from uncertainty, fluidity, and complexity.

Pursuing effective reconstruction within contexts of conflict and fragility is a process for minimizing these frictions while protecting vulnerable people and creating the conditions for peace and stability. Based on the lessons from Iraq, how can the international community enhance the effectiveness of reconstruction? This study offers four recommendations for the international community and external actors engaged in reconstruction activities in the future. Two are principles for guiding their actions, and two are agendas for finding better mechanisms to address reconstruction.

First, the international community needs to prioritize reinforcing national success through national institutions. Imposing what the international community considered success, without giving due consideration to the local constraints and challenges or to the need for sufficient engagement from national institutions, did not work in Iraq. On the contrary, imposing external solutions can provoke counterproductive reactions, no matter how effective the solutions may appear.

This study highlights several elements in undertaking this approach. In particular, donors and international organizations are advised to undertake the following:

- Draw out and strengthen internal abilities within national institutions and avoid trying to replace existing capacities

- Reinforce inclusiveness in national institutions and help to cultivate the representation of diverse needs

- Reinforce accountability in the relationship between national institutions and citizens

- Support national institutions, communities, and citizens in reinforcing social capital.

Second, international domestic decision makers need to balance interventions of varying time and scale according to country needs. While seizing windows of opportunity to realize quick wins is important, an excessive focus on short-term gains can compromise longer-term success. Such was the case in Iraq's electricity sector, where early U.S. reconstruction efforts proved unsustainable and may have exacerbated later power generation problems. Similarly, while small-scale projects can be attractive for their relatively limited scope and ease of completion, large projects done right can demonstrate far more lasting tangible gains to the local population.

There is no single correct response to these trade-offs, as local contexts and conditions will vary, but the formula needs to be based on whether the approach will help to build public confidence in national institutions and whether it will encourage positive behavioral change in local partners.

Third, the international community needs a better mechanism for supporting private sector activities in conflict and fragile settings. Without promoting private sector activities that create broader economic opportunities, the success of reconstruction efforts will be limited. In Iraq, the most critical shortcoming in reconstruction was that it failed to diversify the Iraqi economy away from the dominant oil sector; as a result, few economic opportunities were created in the non-oil private sector. The biggest obstacle, of course, has been the dire security situation, which has discouraged both foreign and local private actors from investing and expanding their business activities. The role of the private sector has remained that of contractor for government- and donor-funded projects. This role is closely associated with the relationship between profitability and risks. Although risks are high, private investment in profitable sectors still occurs, as engagement in Iraq's oil sector has shown. The international community may be limited in what it can do to improve the profitability of each business, but it might be able to find better mechanisms for lowering risk.

Fourth, the international community needs to find an effective mechanism for integrating the actors and efforts of the security and development spheres. In conflict-affected states, lack of security presents the most serious challenge for reconstruction activities. Security and reconstruction as well as development are inextricably linked: reconstruction and development cannot take place in a security vacuum; likewise, security cannot be assured in the absence of successful reconstruction and development. In Iraq, the failure of the two domains to coordinate effectively left in place the conditions for repeated cycles of violence. It is time for the international community to come up with a new mechanism for responding to both the security and development challenges of reconstruction operations.

Methodology

This study is based on reports and data compiled by the Iraqi government, the United Nations, U.S. government agencies, the World Bank, and other concerned parties involved in the reconstruction of Iraq. As more than 15 years have passed since the invasion, some relevant data and information are no longer available. However, interviews were conducted with former officials of the CPA, the Iraqi government, the United Nations, the U.S. Agency for International Development, the U.S. Department of Defense, the U.S. Department of State, the World Bank, bilateral donors, NGOs, and both international and Iraqi contractors and consultants. Interviews were conducted in Iraq, Jordan, and Lebanon and in Japan and the United States. The findings from the literature reviews were triangulated through these interviews. In addition, this study underwent peer review by several individuals who were deeply engaged in the reconstruction of Iraq for years.

References

CSO (Central Statistical Organization), KRSO (Kurdistan Region Statistics Organization), and United Nations. 2011. *Iraq—Household Socio-Economic Survey for 2011*. Baghdad: CSO, KRSO, and United Nations.

CSO (Central Statistical Organization), KRSO (Kurdistan Region Statistics Organization), and World Bank. 2007. *Iraq—Household Socio-Economic Survey for 2007*. Baghdad: CSO, KRSO, and World Bank.

———. 2011. *Iraq—Knowledge Network Survey for 2011*. Baghdad: CSO, KRSO, and World Bank.

SIGIR (Special Inspector General for Iraq Reconstruction). 2013. *Learning from Iraq: A Final Report from the Special Inspector General for Iraq Reconstruction*. Washington, DC: SIGIR, March. https://www.globalsecurity.org/military/library/report/2013/sigir-learning-from-iraq.pdf.

von Clausewitz, Carl. (1832) 1976. *On War*, trans. Michael Howard and Peter Paret. Princeton, NJ: Princeton University Press.

World Bank. 2017. *Iraq Systematic Country Diagnostic*. Washington, DC: World Bank.

CHAPTER 1

Reconstruction Challenges in Iraq

Introduction

Pursuing effective reconstruction within contexts of conflict and fragility is a formidable challenge. After World War II, the Marshall Plan in Europe and the reconstruction of Japan represented monumental successes in reconstruction. Apart from these experiences, however, it is difficult to find a story of unqualified reconstruction success, especially in the years since the end of the Cold War. One critical difference between these post–World War II experiences and contemporary reconstruction is that recent reconstruction has been undertaken in volatile conditions, and there is not yet a textbook approach to reconstruction activities in fragile and conflict-affected settings.

Reconstruction in fragile and conflict settings is characterized by uncertainty, fluidity, and complexity. Conditions are not static, but dynamic and nonlinear; political, economic, security, and social aspects are always changing. Successful reconstruction in such contexts requires figuring out how to manage uncertain, fluid, and complex situations and how to respond and adapt to these challenges. Amid such difficulties, the international community may hesitate to engage in robust reconstruction activities, but the cost of inaction can be great. The success or failure of country-level reconstruction efforts can have a significant impact on the peace and stability of the broader global community. So how can we manage the process effectively?

To find a more effective approach for future efforts, we need to learn from past reconstruction experiences. The reconstruction of Iraq after 2003 offers many lessons. Between 2003 and 2014, more than

US$220 billion was spent on reconstruction efforts following the United States–led invasion and overthrow of the Saddam Hussein regime, but the reconstruction experience has been highly criticized, both within the international community and in Iraq itself. More recently, after years of fighting the Islamic State of Iraq and the Levant (ISIL), also known as Daesh—whose emergence many observers attribute to the failures of reconstruction in the wake of the Iraq War—the international community and the Iraqi government must again begin planning for a new wave of reconstruction.

This study draws lessons and provides recommendations for future reconstruction activities in fragile countries by examining reconstruction in Iraq from 2003 until May 2014, just before the emergence of Daesh. Iraq's reconstruction between 2003 to 2014 was marked by several phases according to changing political, social, and security circumstances (annex 1A). Despite the tens of billions of dollars spent since 2003, the Iraqi people continue to face many challenges: the daily threat of violence, poor public services, widespread corruption, and growing political and social divisions. The question of what went wrong in Iraq has been the topic of many books, articles, and academic papers. Most analyses address U.S. policies, military intervention, and Iraqi politics, while reviews of the reconstruction process are often limited to each donor's operation. This study reviews the reconstruction of Iraq more broadly. The case of Iraq offers few successes and many failures from which the international community can learn.

Security

Volatile security conditions posed the most formidable challenge to the Iraqi people, the Iraqi economy, and reconstruction efforts. Although it is difficult to assess the exact number of deaths, at least 180,000 Iraqi civilians are thought to have been killed through insurgent and sectarian violence between March 2003 and February 2017.[1] At the peak of the insurgency between mid-2006 and mid-2007, the number of deaths of Iraqi civilians stood at roughly 3,000 per month, or around 100 per day.

The security situation varied widely over time and across governorates. As indicated in figure1.1, while the Baghdad Governorate had the highest incidence of civilian casualties, security improved significantly after 2008, only to worsen again after 2012. Security in the Basra governorate remained volatile for the first several years after the invasion, but improved significantly after 2008 and, to date, remains relatively stable. In the Anbar Governorate, noted for its volatility in the first several years following the invasion, after a brief respite, security again deteriorated

FIGURE 1.1

Civilian Deaths from Violence in the Anbar, Baghdad, Basra, and Erbil Governorates of Iraq, 2003–16

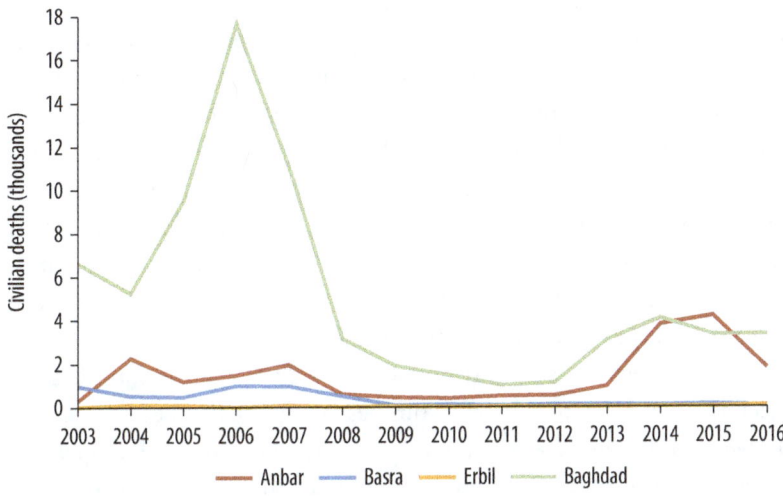

Source: Iraq Body Count data (https://www.iraqbodycount.org/).

beginning in 2013 due to the activities of Daesh. Although the Erbil Governorate was subject to occasional insurgent activities, the region has been largely successful in containing violent activities, which has enabled reconstruction activities to be undertaken with fewer security constraints.

Institutions

Institutional Capacity before 2003

Persons engaged in Iraq's reconstruction right after the invasion in 2003 encountered many experienced Iraqi officials who, for the most part, were in their 50s or 60s. Most of these Iraqi workers had received a good education in their youth, and some had received further training through their employers after graduating from a university. This period during the 1970s and early 1980s has been referred to as "the golden age of Iraqi education," when Iraq's human resources and institutional capacity were among the best in the Middle East and North Africa region, with high levels of public investment and income (Yamao and Sakai 2013, 154).

The combination of a strong education system and abundant job opportunities laid a firm foundation for the Iraqi workforce and institutional capacity, as attested to by the Iraqi recovery after the Gulf War in 1991. The damage to infrastructure was significant following 42 days of continuous air strikes and attacks by coalition forces. Close to 4,000 schools, 260 bridges, hundreds of electricity and petroleum facilities, and many other buildings and infrastructure were destroyed. Despite these difficulties—as well as limited access to spare parts and supplies due to international embargoes and an absence of the foreign expertise that had originally helped to build the country's infrastructure—Iraq managed to restore many facilities without any external support. Yet while the damage caused by the invasion in 2003 was less severe, the Coalition Provisional Authority (CPA) and donors struggled far more in their efforts to restore infrastructure, frustrating many Iraqi officials whose own reconstruction efforts had achieved so much after the Gulf War.

This golden age of Iraqi education gradually ended, with the Iran-Iraq War that raged from 1980 to 1988, the Gulf War in 1991, and ensuing economic sanctions all contributing to its demise. Compounding the decline in education, job opportunities for graduates became scarcer. Between 1991 and 2003, economic activity and government spending were highly restrained and conducted under the supervision of United Nations (UN) observers. Over time, the brain drain of academics and technical workers such as doctors and engineers grew steadily.

The effect of this generation gap between older, educated, and skilled workers and younger Iraqis who have had fewer opportunities for professional growth is becoming ever more serious, as public servants retire and make way for less-experienced successors to occupy senior ministerial posts.

Iraqi Institutions after 2003

Despite the deterioration of Iraqi institutions in the preceding years, by 2003, many experienced Iraqi officials were still in the country, but they were largely sidelined by CPA officials, who favored working with Iraqi exiles over officials who had held government posts before the war (Sky 2015, 11).[2] Institutions were further weakened by the issuance of CPA Order no. 1 on May 16, 2003, which removed the top four ranks of Baath Party officials from government posts. According to Emma Sky, a former political adviser to the U.S. military, "The architect of this policy in Washington had studied the experience of Germany in 1945 and regarded de-Nazification as a model" (Sky 2015, 56, 218). This order led to the firing of around 30,000 ex-Baathists from various ministries, of which 15,000 eventually were permitted to return to work upon appeal (Otterman 2005).

While the brutality of the Saddam regime cannot be questioned, many Baath Party members had belonged to the party for the sake of promotion in government posts and had never committed a serious crime; nevertheless, they were deprived of opportunities to play a key role in future nation-building efforts. This restriction imposed significant constraints on government capacity. Like the decision to dissolve the Iraqi army, de-Baathification likely pushed some Iraqis toward violent resistance who might otherwise have been co-opted into rebuilding the country (Diamond 2004, 44).

Ethnosectarian Diversity and Its Influences over Institutions

The people living in the greater Tigris-Euphrates River Basin, the areas in which the current Iraq is located, hold multiple identities based on the tribes and sectarian and ethnic groups to which they belong. While Iraq has many religious and ethnic minority groups—such as Christian, Turkoman, and Yezidi—the largest and most pronounced ethnosectarian divisions are between three groups: Arab-Shia, Arab-Sunni, and Kurds. Each group is far from monolithic, however, as shown by past episodes of fighting between the two main Kurdistan groups—the Kurdistan Democratic Party and the Patriotic Union of Kurdistan—during the 1990s and by the divisions among Shia communities during the uprising against the Saddam regime after the Gulf War in 1991. The strength of ethnic identity changes frequently, depending on the relationships between the rulers (or the state after 1932) and the people. In Iraqi history, the idea of tribe and tribal leaders has also shifted in response to changes in the identity and capacity of its rulers (Tripp 2002, 2–3).

The state of Iraq was itself only formed in 1921 under the British mandate after the dissolution of the Ottoman Empire, achieving independence, albeit nominally, in 1932. Therefore, the idea of a national Iraqi identity was relatively new, and rulers of the state had to consider this diversity. Under the oppression of Saddam Hussein, the differences in ethnicity, religion, and tribes were less critical. Privileges mainly went to kin affiliates of the Saddam ruling family. Even though non-Sunnis thought that Arab-Sunnis enjoyed privileges under the Saddam regime, most Arab-Sunnis suffered just like the Kurds and Arab-Shia (Al Aqeedi 2017).

After the invasion and collapse of the Saddam regime, however, groups began emphasizing their differences to enhance their political leverage, further intensifying divisions within the country. Each ethnosectarian and political group battled to dominate ministries and local governments, with the result that each government entity became subject to the influence of particular groups. In addition, the politicization of public institutions became closely related to corruption. After the invasion, political parties in Iraq pursued their own economic benefits from government contracts, while certain political leaders manipulated graft investigations for political advantage, eroding the credibility of anticorruption efforts.

Some of the actions taken by the United States–led occupation force may have inadvertently entrenched identity divisions further. For example, the CPA's decision to form the Iraqi Governing Council along ethnosectarian lines may have been well intentioned as a form of affirmative action, but it only served to make distinctions between ethnic groups more pronounced. One senior CPA adviser described how the CPA promoted the most sectarian elements in society, saying "We gather together the representatives of the most antagonistic factions and think that's good democracy. We've done nothing to blur the lines separating people and everything to sharpen them" (Agresto 2007, 1405). Many regional actors—the Islamic Republic of Iran, in particular—exerted significant political influence. While Iraqi institutional capacity was weakened by the political interventions of external actors, weak national institutions created room for ethnosectarian influence over ministries that hampered their effective functioning.

The Economy

The most prominent characteristic of the Iraqi economy is its dependence on oil revenues. The oil sector accounts for 60 percent of gross domestic product (GDP), and oil revenues account for 90 percent of budget revenues. Thus, the Iraqi economy is highly vulnerable to fluctuations in oil prices, production, and exports. In the late 1970s, thanks to increasing oil production and exports as well as higher oil prices, GDP per capita reached US$4,000. During that period, backed by abundant oil revenues, Iraq undertook massive infrastructure development. The start of the war between Iraq and the Islamic Republic of Iran in 1980, compounded by a rapid decline in oil prices, hurt the economy and reversed some of the previous decade's gains. The Gulf War followed in 1991, with the imposition of economic sanctions and a ban on oil exports (figure 1.2). By 1996 Iraqi GDP per capita had dropped to around US$340 (figure 1.3). During the sanctions period, public sector salaries declined to as low as US$3 per month, and livelihoods were sustained mainly by the food rationing system run by the government. In that sense, instead of curbing the authoritarian regime, economic sanctions expanded the role of the state and strengthened its authority over Iraqi citizens, while the country as a whole and the population at large suffered (Mazaheri 2010; Sassoon 2016).

FIGURE 1.2

Oil Production and Exports in Iraq, 1980–2014

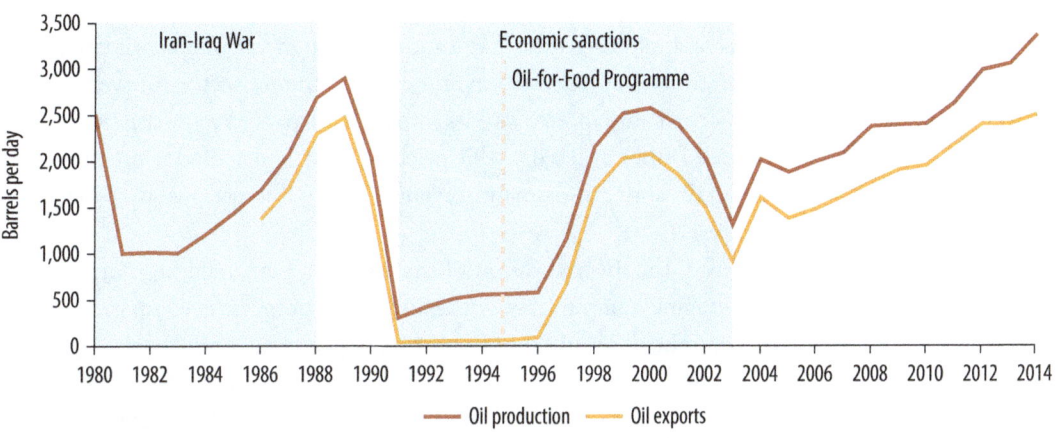

Source: World Bank data.

FIGURE 1.3

GDP per Capita and Crude Oil Prices in Iraq, 1970–2014

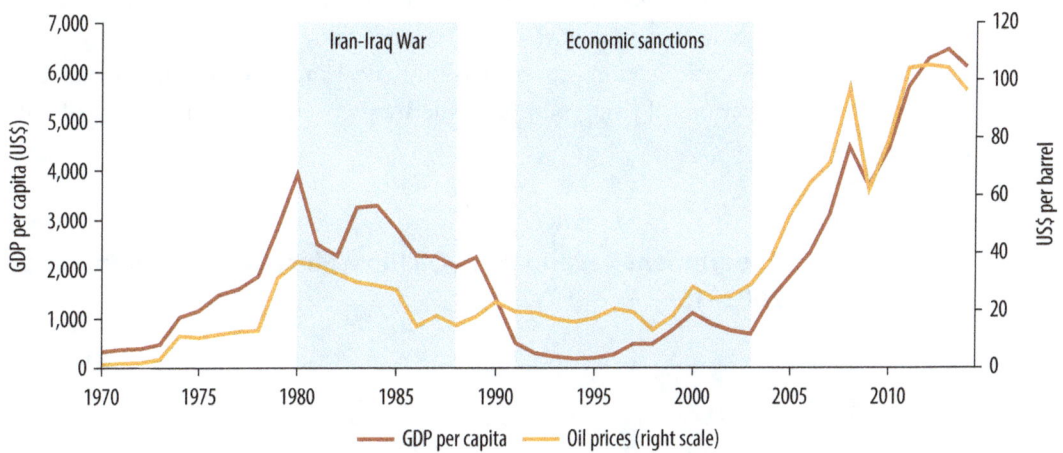

Sources: Economist Intelligence Unit data; World Bank data.

The Economic Challenges of Reconstruction

Iraq confronted diverse economic challenges after 2003. First, unlike some postconflict cases, the reconstruction of Iraq was not concerned merely with ensuring economic recovery to preconflict levels. Damage to infrastructure from military operations during the invasion itself was limited; rather, the deterioration of infrastructure had been well under way long before the invasion. Moreover, economic sanctions and the

Oil-for-Food Programme (OFFP) introduced severe distortions into the economy and its institutions. Thus, a major challenge during the reconstruction of Iraq was to rebuild the economy and infrastructure simultaneously.

Second, although the CPA and the Iraqi government prioritized the restoration of oil production and exports, the oil sector recovered more slowly than anticipated, and its impact on broader reconstruction efforts increased only gradually. Oil prices, in particular, had a greater effect on GDP and government revenues than fluctuations in production (figure 1.4).

Third, the diversification of the economy remained high on the economic agenda of the Iraqi government, but progress even up to today has been minimal. While the economy's dependence on oil makes it highly vulnerable to fluctuations in oil prices, the capital-intensive oil sector employs only 1–2 percent of Iraq's labor force. Oil revenues provide abundant resources to enable the government to be a major provider of employment opportunities, but government employment heavily burdens the fiscal system and makes the budget system inflexible. Separately, because of the high concentration of resources, sectors unrelated to oil have developed little. Meanwhile, the uneven geographic distribution of oil resources has fueled regional and sectarian disputes. These challenges are typical consequences of a "resource curse."

Fourth, institutions created bottlenecks for reconstruction activities. In periods of rising oil prices, the Iraqi government was able to allocate

FIGURE 1.4

Government Revenue and Oil Price Fluctuations in Iraq, 2003–15

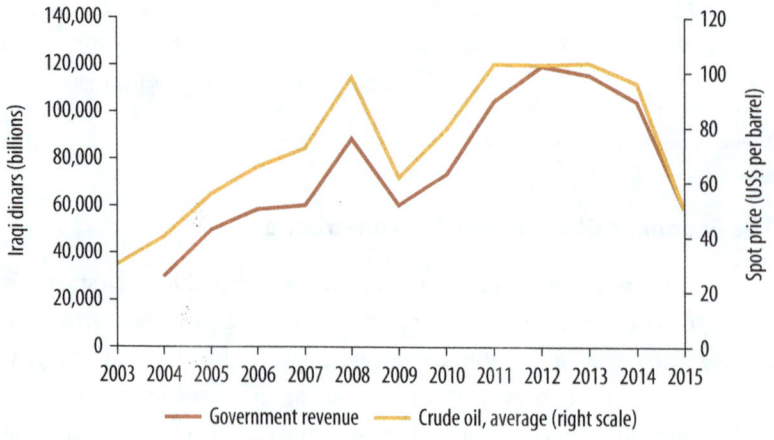

Source: International Monetary Fund data.

substantial resources to capital investment projects and reconstruction activities, but the budget execution rate remained low, at around 40–60 percent (figure 1.5). This suggests that institutional capacity, rather than a lack of financial resources, hindered reconstruction activities.

Fifth, high expectations for private investment in Iraq when military activities drew to a close were realized only in the oil sector; in non-oil sectors, both foreign and domestic private investment remained limited. For all the efforts of the post-Saddam administrations, the Iraqi economy continued to operate largely under state control. Although a growing number of new private companies emerged during the course of reconstruction, Iraq's private sector remains dominated by individual, micro, and small companies owned by sole proprietors or family partnerships, and their impact on the economy and nationwide employment opportunities has been modest (PMAC 2014). Accelerating the development of the Iraqi private sector, especially non-oil sectors, is indispensable for job creation and the future growth of Iraq's economy.

Foreign direct investment, outside of the oil sector, comes mostly from private companies based within the region, particularly those from the Gulf States and Turkey. A combination of constraints—such as poor security, dire infrastructure, volatile political conditions, and corruption—continues to make private parties from outside the region reluctant to invest in Iraq's non-oil sectors.

FIGURE 1.5

Investment Budget Execution in Iraq, 2005–13

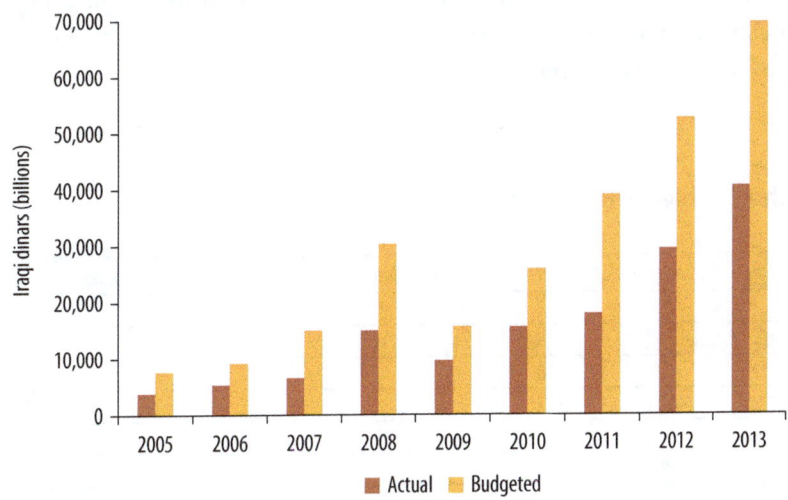

Source: Iraq Ministry of Finance, quoted in World Bank 2014.

Unemployment during Reconstruction

Job creation was one of the highest reconstruction priorities after the invasion in 2003. Polls conducted in early 2004 showed that a majority of Iraqis considered unemployment to be a serious problem (table 1.1).

An initial problem involved ascertaining the actual unemployment rate, with estimates varying wildly due to differing definitions of unemployment and a lack of reliable data, especially regarding the informal sector and the number of ghost workers. A survey by the United Nations Development Programme of living conditions in Iraq in 2004 estimated unemployment—calculated based on the International Labour Organization methodology—at about 10.5 percent (IMF 2005); more worrying, it estimated a 37 percent unemployment rate among the educated young, including discouraged workers. Estimates from the Iraq Ministry of Planning put the overall unemployment rate much higher (28 percent), as did CPA estimates (30 percent) and those compiled by scholars at the Brookings Institution (30–45 percent) and Baghdad University (70 percent) (IMF 2005).

The public sector has been the dominant formal employer in Iraq for decades. Abundant oil revenue allowed the government to provide jobs for the majority of workers—a dynamic that, before the invasion, formed a key pillar of the social contract between Saddam's regime and the Iraqi people. The private sector was undeveloped and employed a small fraction of the labor force. After the invasion, many donors and international organizations engaged in job creation programs, but most efforts focused on temporary employment. Public sector employment grew larger, becoming increasingly nonmeritocratic, and the sector has come to be viewed as a de facto social safety net for Iraqis. Between 2003 and 2015, the core public sector expanded from 900,000 employees to more than 3 million, providing approximately 42 percent of all jobs (figure 1.6). Public employee salaries became the largest expenditure item in the government budget (figure 1.7).

TABLE 1.1

Public Perceptions of the Problems Facing Iraq, February 2004

% of respondents

Problem	Very good	Quite good	Quite bad	Very bad	Not sure or no answer	Not applicable	Total
The security situation	20.2	28.7	21.1	29.0	1.0	0.0	100
The availability of jobs	6.5	19.1	22.5	46.1	5.8	0.0	100
The supply of electricity	7.9	27.0	27.8	36.6	0.7	0.0	100
The availability of clean water	19.7	30.8	21.7	26.3	1.5	0.0	100
The availability of medical care	16.9	34.1	24.4	21.8	2.0	0.8	100
Local schools	36.6	34.6	15.0	11.1	2.4	0.4	100
Local government	17.8	31.7	20.4	17.7	12.4	0.0	100

Source: Oxford Research International 2004.

FIGURE 1.6

Core Public Sector Employment in Iraq, 2003–15

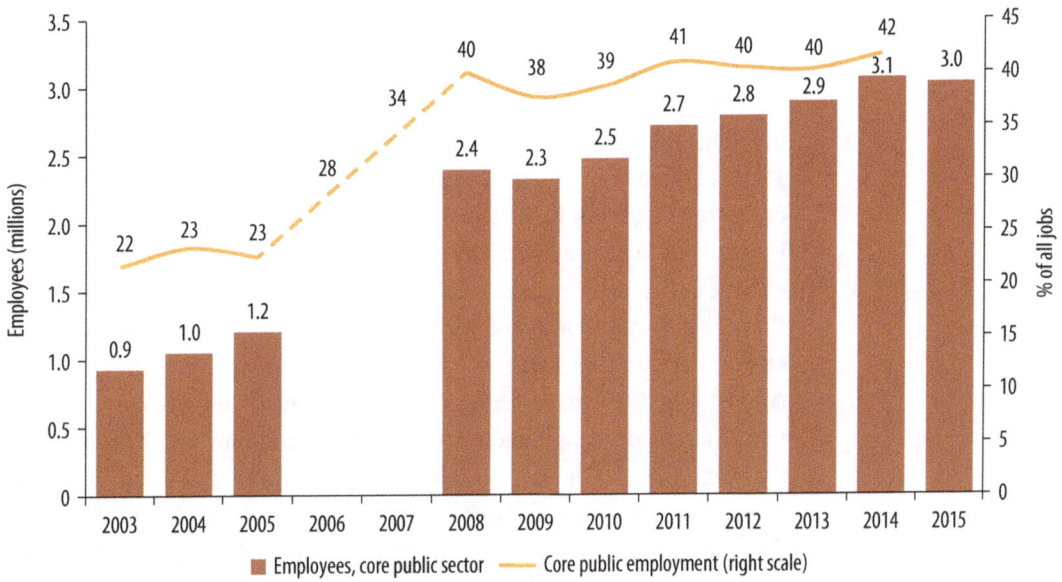

Sources: Iraq Ministry of Finance data; World Development Indicators data, quoted in World Bank 2017b.

FIGURE 1.7

Average Composition of Public Expenditures in Iraq, 2005–10

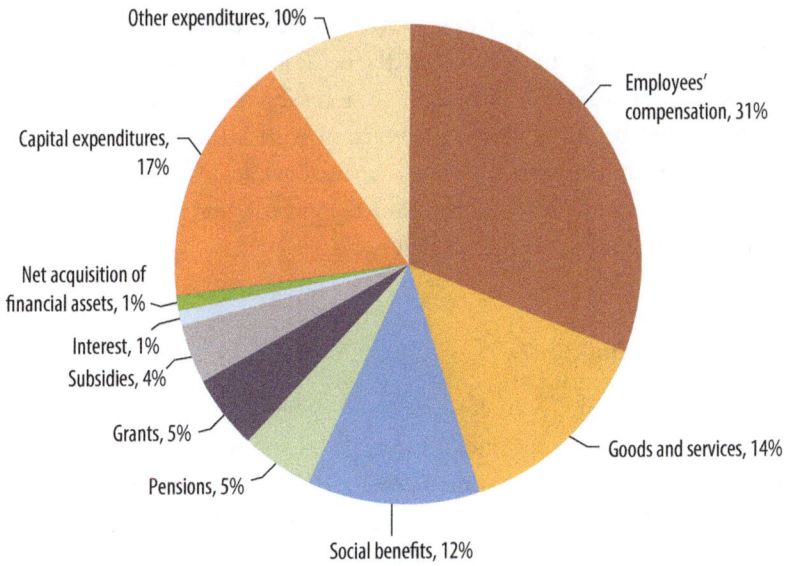

Source: World Bank 2014.

Annex 1A: Phases of Iraqi Reconstruction, March 2003 to June 2014

March 2003 to June 2004

Immediately after the invasion, Iraq was placed under the administration of a foreign power, and Iraqi institutions were marginalized in initial nation-building efforts. The United Nations Security Council (UNSC) Resolution 1483, adopted May 22, 2003, empowered the United States–led coalition, under the Coalition Provisional Authority, as the de facto government in Iraq for the first year of occupation. The CPA led most reconstruction efforts, and its senior advisers for each sector held authority equivalent to that of ministers. Compared with later years, levels of violence were moderate, although an attack on the UN headquarters in Baghdad on August 19, 2003, made it clear that the norms of aid worker neutrality would not be observed. Because of the attack, combined with the ambiguity of its roles under the occupation, the UN decided to remove its staff from Iraq, and many bilateral organizations followed suit. Although donors and international organizations physically withdrew from the country, they continued to provide assistance remotely. The United Kingdom and the United States, meanwhile, remained and continued reconstruction activities within the country. A political milestone took place in March 2004, when the Transitional Administrative Law (TAL)—the provisional Constitution—was drafted and approved by the CPA and the Iraq Governing Council, an advisory body established by the CPA and consisting of 25 Iraqi political and tribal leaders.

During this phase, all donors and international organizations had difficulty grasping needs on the ground, partly because of the absence of a sovereign government and partly because of a lack of assessment and sector strategy and planning. As a result, projects and programs were selected based on limited interaction with Iraqi counterparts and in an opportunistic manner. Many international actors were engaged in procurement and delivery of goods or equipment, and others in ad hoc emergency repairs to existing facilities.

July 2004 to Mid-2007

In accordance with UNSC Resolution 1546, the CPA transferred sovereignty back to Iraq at the end of June 2004, handing caretaker authority over to the interim government led by Prime Minister Ayad Allawi. In line with TAL provisions, parliamentary elections for the 275-member transitional National Assembly of Iraq were held on January 30, 2005. In May 2005, the newly elected assembly selected a transitional government, to be led by Prime Minister Ibrahim al-Jaffari, and was given a mandate to write a permanent Constitution for Iraq. Drafted by committee, the Constitution was ratified by a national referendum on October 15, 2005. The first official general election to elect a permanent National Assembly was held on December 15, 2005, although it would take another five months to select Nouri al-Maliki as prime minister. On May 20, 2006, al-Maliki's cabinet was sworn in as the first full-fledged government of postwar Iraq.

While most international organizations and bilateral donors, aside from the United Kingdom and the United States, had left Iraq by the spring of 2004, some international NGOs retained a presence in the country and were still able to move around Iraq relatively unrestricted and without the need for visible security. However, as attacks on and kidnapping of aid workers grew, international NGOs began withdrawing from Iraq, while coalition staff mobility became highly constrained. The situation continued to deteriorate, and at the peak of insurgent activities, from June 2006 to May 2007, the monthly toll of civilian deaths averaged 2,843. Reconstruction activities had to be managed remotely either from neighboring countries or from the International Zone of Baghdad. With security concerns at crisis levels, the United States developed a new strategy in January 2007 to increase the number of troops deployed to the country.

During this phase, donors and international organizations were challenged by their ambition to pursue more substantial reconstruction activities while being unable to operate ground activities freely for their implementation. While training offered outside of the country increased donor interaction with Iraqis, managing operations remotely and providing additional security in-country caused project and program costs to skyrocket.

Mid-2007 to the End of 2010

As the U.S. military surge came into effect in early 2007, military operations were undertaken jointly with Sunni tribal security forces—the so-called "Sahwa" or "Sons of Iraq"—and security conditions began to improve. In 2008, the U.S. administration under President George. W. Bush and the Iraqi government signed the United States–Iraq Status of Forces Agreement, which stated that U.S. troops would withdraw after three years—by the end of 2011—and hand sovereignty over security back to the Iraqi government, a risky but nonetheless politically important measure.

National Assembly elections were held in March 2010, resulting in a partial victory for the Iraqi National Movement, led by former Interim

FIGURE 1A.1

Oil Production, Electricity Generation, and Iraqi Investment Expenditures, 2002–13

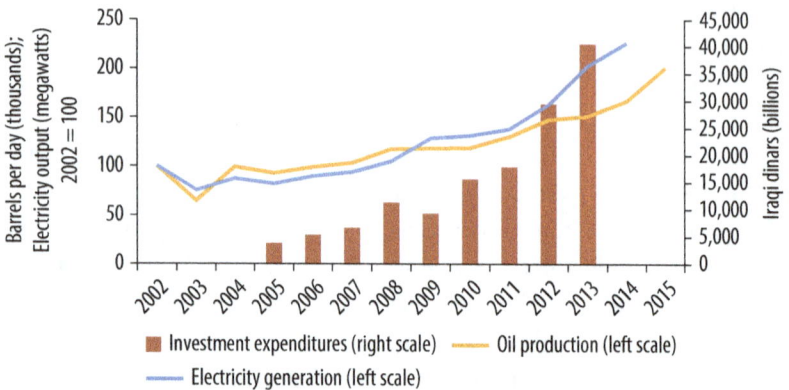

Sources: Information from the Iraq Ministry of Electricity, the Iraq Ministry of Finance, and the U.S. Energy Information Administration; World Bank 2017a.
Note: The exchange rate for the Iraqi dinar has been pegged to around ID 1,170 = US$1 since 2008.

Prime Minister Ayad Allawi, winning a total of 91 seats and making it the largest alliance in the National Assembly. The State of Law Coalition, led by incumbent Prime Minister Nouri al-Maliki, made up the second-largest group, with 89 seats. After nine months of intensive negotiations, it was agreed that al-Maliki would continue to serve as prime minister, and in December 2010, his second administration was sworn in.

With improving security and a degree of political stability, aid workers began returning to Iraq, and reconstruction activities finally began to show results. For example, electricity generation and oil output, which had been hovering around prewar levels, began to improve gradually (figure 1A.1). But by this point, momentum for the provision of support for Iraq's reconstruction had ebbed, and donors offered only limited new assistance.

2011 to June 2014

In December 2011, the United States completed its withdrawal of troops. Meanwhile, there was growing criticism of the prime minister for concentrating executive power in his own hands. Political tensions among different political parties and sectarian groups were growing, especially after an arrest warrant was issued for a vice president and prominent Sunni politician. At the same time, tensions were mounting between the central government and the Kurdistan Regional Government (KRG), as international oil companies began working directly with the KRG in the north, while the KRG complained of problems with the central government's budget transfer process and pursued efforts to gain more autonomy under the federal system.

Security remained relatively stable until the middle of 2013 but started to deteriorate again when militia and insurgent groups began exploiting political and ethnosectarian divisions as well as deficiencies in the Iraqi security forces. Events reached a low point when the terrorist group Daesh captured the city of Mosul on June 10, 2014. At the same time, a rapid drop in the price of oil hit Iraqi government revenues hard, and the rehabilitation of infrastructure, which had continued steadily despite the deteriorating security and political environment, ground to a halt.

Notes

1. According to data compiled by the Iraqi Body Count database, as of March 2017 (https://iraqbodycount.org/).
2. As Sky puts it, "Bremer did not believe there were credible Iraqi leaders who could assume power, and he decided that the CPA had to directly administer the country for an undefined period. America was going to rebuild Iraq, as it had rebuilt Germany and Japan after World War II."

References

Agresto, John. 2007. *Mugged by Reality*. New York: Encounter Books.

Al Aqeedi, Rasha. 2017. "Disarray among Iraqi Sunnis Yields Opportunity for Nationalism." *The Century Foundation* (Commentary), April 26. https://tcf.org/content/commentary/disarray-among-iraqi-sunnis-yields-opportunity-nationalism/.

Diamond, Larry. 2004. "What Went Wrong in Iraq." *Foreign Affairs* 83 (5): 34–56.

IMF (International Monetary Fund). 2005. *Iraq: Article IV Consultation*. Country Report 05/294. Washington, DC: IMF.

Mazaheri, Nima. 2010. "Iraq and the Domestic Political Effects of Economic Sanctions." *Middle East Journal* 64 (2): 253–68.

Otterman, Sharon. 2005. "Debaathification." *Council on Foreign Relations*, February 22. https://www.cfr.org/backgrounder/iraq-debaathification.

Oxford Research International. 2004. *National Survey of Iraq: February 2004*. Oxford: Oxford Research International. http://news.bbc.co.uk/nol/shared/bsp/hi/pdfs/15_03_04_iraqsurvey.pdf.

PMAC (Prime Minister's Advisory Commission). 2014. *Private Sector Development Strategy 2014–2030*. Baghdad: PMAC. http://cabinet.iq/uploads/pdf/2015-3/2.pdf.

Sassoon, Joseph. 2016. "Iraq's Political Economy Post 2003: From Transition to Corruption." *International Journal of Contemporary Iraqi Studies* 10 (1-2): 17–33.

Sky, Emma. 2015. *The Unraveling: High Hopes and Missed Opportunities in Iraq*. New York: Public Affairs.

Tripp, Charles. 2002. *A History of Iraq*. Cambridge: Cambridge University Press.

World Bank. 2014. *Republic of Iraq: Public Expenditure Review*. Washington, DC: World Bank.

———. 2017a. *Iraq Public Expenditure Review*. Washington, DC: World Bank.

———. 2017b. *Iraq Systematic Country Diagnostic*. Washington, DC: World Bank.

Yamao, Dai, and Keiko Sakai. 2013. *60 Chapters to Understand the Contemporary Iraq* [in Japanese]. Tokyo: Akashi Shobo.

CHAPTER 2

International Engagement in the Reconstruction of Iraq

Overview of International Actors

Beginning in 2003, diverse and significant actors, both domestic and international, engaged in reconstruction activities in Iraq. At the Madrid Donor Conference in October 2003, the international community—represented by 38 countries, the European Commission, the International Monetary Fund (IMF), and the World Bank—announced overall and indicative pledges amounting to more than US$33 billion in grants and loans (figure 2.1).

The international community established a trust fund called the International Reconstruction Fund Facility for Iraq (IRFFI) as an international financial mechanism for reconstruction activities. The fund had two windows: the World Bank Iraq Trust Fund (WBITF), and the United Nations Development Group Iraq Trust Fund (UNDGITF). This was the first time that the United Nations (UN) and the World Bank had jointly managed a trust fund. Donors committed US$1.86 billion, making it the second-largest postcrisis multidonor trust fund up to that point (table 2.1). Seventeen donors deposited a total of US$497 million into the WBITF to support 22 projects, while 25 donors deposited a total of US$1.358 billion into the UNDGITF to support 200 projects (Scanteam 2009, 1).

Over the course of reconstruction, however, the size of support grew significantly—particularly the U.S. commitments, which amounted to US$18.6 billion at the Madrid conference but grew to US$60 billion, including around US$27 billion for security-related expenditures,

FIGURE 2.1

Pledges Made at the International Donor Conference for Iraq Reconstruction, October 2003

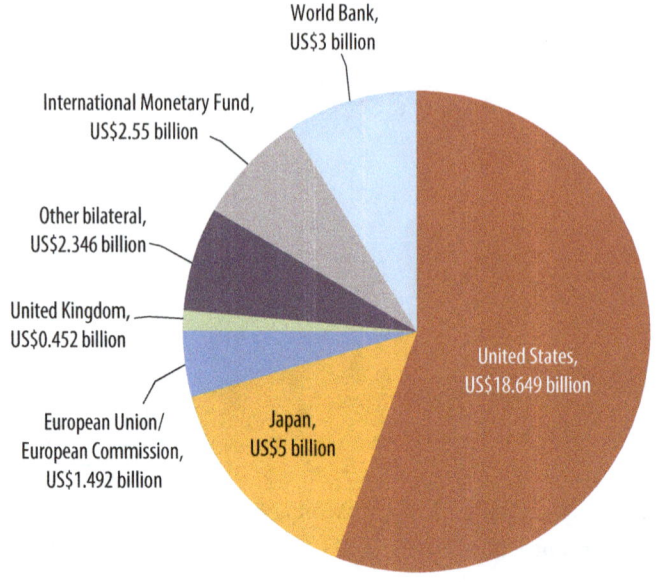

Total pledged: US$33 billion

Source: United Nations Development Programme.

TABLE 2.1

Total Donor Contributions to the International Reconstruction Fund Facility for Iraq (IRFFI)

US$ (thousands)

Donor	UNDPITF	WBITF	Total
European Commission	594,210	179,740	773,950
Japan	360,951	130,600	491,551
Spain	93,173	20,000	113,173
Canada	63,785	26,700	90,485
United Kingdom	55,542	71,400	126,942
Italy	39,232		39,232
Australia	31,663	16,140	47,803
Korea, Rep.	21,000	9,000	30,000
Sweden	13,657	5,800	19,457
Denmark	12,410		12,410
Germany	10,000		10,000
Finland	7,700	2,600	10,300
Norway	7,009	6,700	13,709
Netherlands	6,697	6,200	12,897
India	5,000	5,000	10,000

(continued on next page)

TABLE 2.1

Total Donor Contributions to the International Reconstruction Fund Facility for Iraq (IRFFI) (*continued*)

Donor	UNDPITF	WBITF	Total
Kuwait	5,000	5,000	10,000
Qatar	5,000	5,000	10,000
United States	5,000	5,000	10,000
Turkey	9,000	1,000	10,000
Greece	3,630		3,630
New Zealand	3,365		3,365
Luxembourg	2,319		2,319
Belgium	1,321		1,321
Ireland	1,226		1,226
Iceland	500	1,000	1,500
Total deposits	1,358,390	496,880	1,855,270

Source: Scanteam 2009.
Note: UNDGITF = United Nations Development Group Iraq Trust Fund; WBITF = World Bank Iraq Trust Fund.

FIGURE 2.2

Funding Sources for Iraq Reconstruction, 2003–12

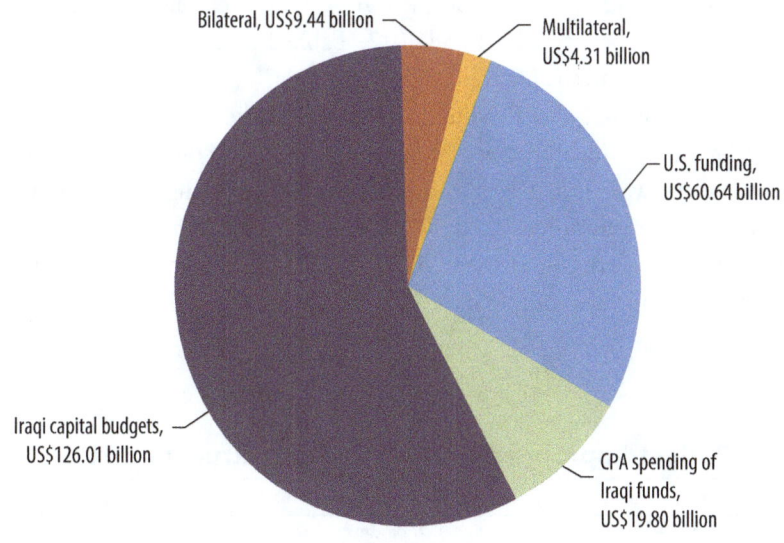

Source: SIGIR 2013.
Note: Total: US$220 billion. CPA = Coalition Provisional Authority.

such as training and equipping Iraqi security forces. As Iraqi oil production and exports began to recover, a substantial amount of Iraq's capital investment was allocated to reconstruction activities. The total financial commitment for the reconstruction of Iraq amounted to US$220.1 billion by the end of 2012 (figure 2.2).

Key Actors in the International Response

The U.S. Role in Reconstruction

In the first few years after the invasion, the United States led all actors in the amount of resources committed to and the role performed in Iraq's reconstruction. To oversee reconstruction activities, the U.S. Office of Reconstruction and Humanitarian Assistance (ORHA) was established before the invasion; after United Nations Security Council (UNSC) Resolution 1483 empowered the United States–led occupation force with executive, judicial, and legislative authority to govern Iraq, this role was taken over by the Coalition Provisional Authority (CPA) in May 2003. The CPA was the central player in Iraq's reconstruction until sovereignty was transferred to the Iraqi interim government in June 2004. Still, even after handing over sovereignty, the United States continued to be a major actor in reconstruction activities.

Initial estimates put the cost of Iraq's reconstruction to U.S. taxpayers at US$1.7 billion (SIGIR 2009, 51). This proved to be a gross underestimate; according to the report of the Special Inspector General for Iraq Reconstruction (SIGIR), U.S. spending amounted to US$60 billion between 2003 and 2012. Table 2.2 shows the major U.S. budget appropriations for Iraq's reconstruction.

In addition, UNSC Resolution 1483 established the Development Fund for Iraq, which became the repository for Iraq's oil and natural gas revenue and was estimated to total US$20.7 billion during the 14 months of CPA administration (SIGIR 2013). Resources from the Development Fund for Iraq were complemented by US$2.7 billion in seized and vested assets of the former Iraqi regime.

TABLE 2.2

U.S. Budget Appropriations for Iraq Reconstruction Efforts

Name of fund	Amount (US$, billions)
Iraq Relief and Reconstruction Fund I (April 2003 approval)	2.48
Iraq Relief and Reconstruction Fund II (November 2003 approval)	18.60
Iraq Security Forces Fund	20.19
Economic Support Fund	5.13
Commander's Emergency Response Program	4.12
International Narcotics Control and Law Enforcement account	1.31
Other programs	8.17
Total	60.00

Source: SIGIR 2013.

Organizational Structure of U.S. Reconstruction Operations

The organizational structure of U.S. reconstruction efforts was complex and involved many public and private entities. These entities included the U.S. Agency for International Development (USAID), U.S. Army Corps of Engineers (USACE), U.S. Department of Defense, U.S. Department of State, several newly established entities—for example, the CPA, ORHA, and the Project Management Office (PMO)—the Iraq Reconstruction Management Office (IRMO), the Project Contracting Office (PCO), and American private contractors. Lines of authority and command were intertwined and lacked clarity, creating tensions and confusion among the different actors. These coordination problems were complicated further by the diverse lines of funding made available to each entity.[1]

The U.S. Department of Defense was the de facto lead agency in most reconstruction activities in the first year of reconstruction, and its influence remained strong, albeit diminishing gradually, after dissolution of the CPA in June 2004. U.S. security entities played key roles, both in efforts to rebuild Iraq's security sector and institutions and in other reconstruction activities normally undertaken by development actors.

Amid the worsening security situation, restoring and maintaining the rule of law quickly became the top reconstruction priority for both international and domestic actors. The United States made the largest commitments in this area, including for training and equipping Iraqi security forces and for building capacity in the Iraq Ministry of Defense and Ministry of Interior. These efforts were paid for using different financing resources (table 2.3), with the total security sector budget amounting to more than US$27 billion.

TABLE 2.3

Security and the Rule of Law, Cumulative U.S. Obligations as of September 30, 2012

Type of budget	Amount US$ (billions)
Iraq Security Force Fund	19.57
Iraq Relief and Reconstruction Fund	5.67
International Narcotics and Law Enforcement	1.16
Commander's Emergency Response Program	0.68
Economic Support Fund	0.23
Total	27.31

Source: SIGIR 2013.

U.S. security actors also played a role in reconstruction activities not related to security. For example, the Commander's Emergency Response Program (CERP) provided immediate reconstruction and humanitarian assistance at the local level to support the work of U.S. military commanders. Meanwhile, the Provincial Reconstruction Team program, originally developed in Afghanistan, established a system in which military and civilian personnel sought to work as an integrated team in each governorate. Its mission encompassed not only capacity development efforts to aid provincial and local governments but also projects to support stability operations and the counterinsurgency effort.

Some of these activities have attracted criticism. For example, SIGIR and others have questioned the CERP's lack of a mechanism for measuring the outputs and outcomes of its activities comparable to assessments undertaken by development actors. Separately, the high turnover of military personnel in Iraq affected the management and oversight of CERP projects, and too little provision was made for handing over projects to Iraqi counterparts responsible for ensuring their sustainability (Tarnoff 2009, 18).

Findings from SIGIR

Despite the huge amount of money spent and the large number of projects and programs carried out, U.S. reconstruction efforts in Iraq have been subject to heavy criticism. On the ground, substantial numbers of dedicated U.S. civilian and military personnel were devoted to reconstruction, many of them risking, and some losing, their lives in the process. The question of what went wrong with U.S. reconstruction operations has been the topic of many books, reports, and articles, among which a series of reports produced by SIGIR provided useful information for this research. In 2012, SIGIR conducted extensive interviews with Iraqi ministers and senior officials, as well as with senior U.S. officials and lawmakers familiar with the U.S. reconstruction program in Iraq (SIGIR 2013, 10–14). According to SIGIR's final report, interviewees identified three significant problems:

- The United States failed to consult sufficiently with Iraqi authorities when planning the reconstruction program.

- Corruption and poor security fundamentally impeded progress throughout the program.

- The overall rebuilding effort had only a limited positive effect on conditions on the ground.

SIGIR (2013, xii) identified key lessons for future U.S. reconstruction programs:

- Create an integrated civilian-military office to plan, execute, and be accountable for contingency rebuilding activities during stabilization and reconstruction operations

- Begin rebuilding only after establishing sufficient security and focusing first on small projects and programs

- Ensure full host-country engagement in program and project selection, securing commitments to share costs (possibly through loans) and agreements to sustain completed projects after their transfer

- Establish uniform contracting, personnel, and information management systems that all participants in stabilization and reconstruction operations use

- Require robust oversight of stabilization and reconstruction activities from the operation's inception

- Preserve and refine programs developed in Iraq that produced successes when used judiciously, such as the CERP and the Provincial Reconstruction Team program

- Plan in advance, plan comprehensively and in an integrated fashion, and have backup plans ready to go.

Other Bilateral Donor Assistance for the Reconstruction of Iraq

Many bilateral donors outside of the United States committed large sums of money and took part in various reconstruction activities, albeit on a smaller scale than the United States. Even the United Kingdom, a key coalition partner in the invasion in 2003, wielded only limited influence over the course of reconstruction.

What set other bilateral donors apart was that they advocated for a multilateral approach. The United Kingdom was among the strongest advocates of this approach and of the importance of having the UN and international financial institutions take the lead in the reconstruction process, going so far as proposing, albeit unsuccessfully, that the IMF and the World Bank manage the Development Fund for Iraq. Consistent with this approach, the United Kingdom's initial pledge of £330 million (US$574 million) was diverted to multiple international actors (figure 2.3). By 2010, U.K. development and humanitarian assistance totaled £297 million (US$516 million) and £209 million (US$364 million), respectively.[2]

FIGURE 2.3

Allocation of the U.K. Budget for Iraq's Reconstruction, 2003–July 2004

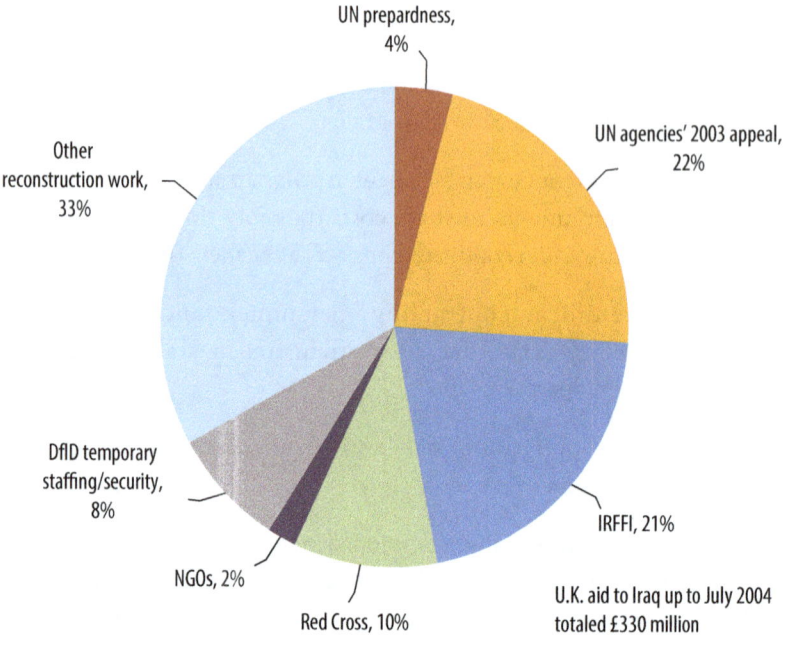

Source: International Development Committee, House of Commons 2005.
Note: UN = United Nations; IRFFI = International Reconstruction Fund Facility for Iraq; NGOs = nongovernmental organizations; DfID = U.K. Department for International Development.

The European Union (EU) was another key donor encouraging a multilateral approach. EU support for Iraq from 2003 to the end of 2013 amounted to around €1 billion (US$1.31 billion), as shown in figure 2.4, which included both reconstruction and humanitarian assistance.[3] Instead of engaging in direct assistance of the type provided by Japan, the United Kingdom, and the United States, EU support for Iraq was channeled through international organizations, such as the UN and other humanitarian agencies, including the International Committee of the Red Cross and international nongovernmental organizations (NGOs). The EU was also the biggest supporter of the IRFFI, with a contribution of roughly US$774 million for both the UN and World Bank windows, which constituted 42 percent of total contributions to the fund.

After the United States, Japan was the largest donor to the reconstruction of Iraq (figure 2.5). At the Madrid Donor Conference in October 2003, the Government of Japan announced an assistance package worth a total of US$5 billion, consisting of US$1.5 billion in grants and US$3.5 billion in concessional loans. Japanese aid was

FIGURE 2.4

Annual European Union Commitment for Development and Humanitarian Assistance to Iraq, 2003–13

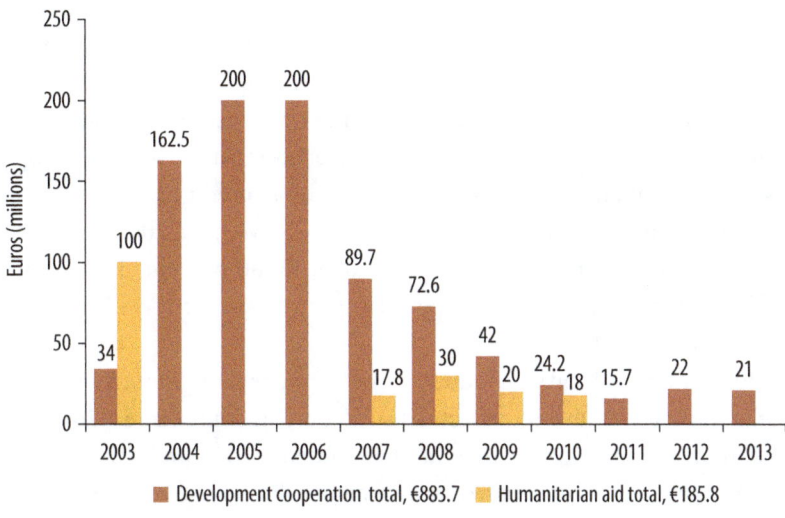

Source: EU 2010.

FIGURE 2.5

Allocation of Japanese Grant Assistance to Iraq, 2003–09

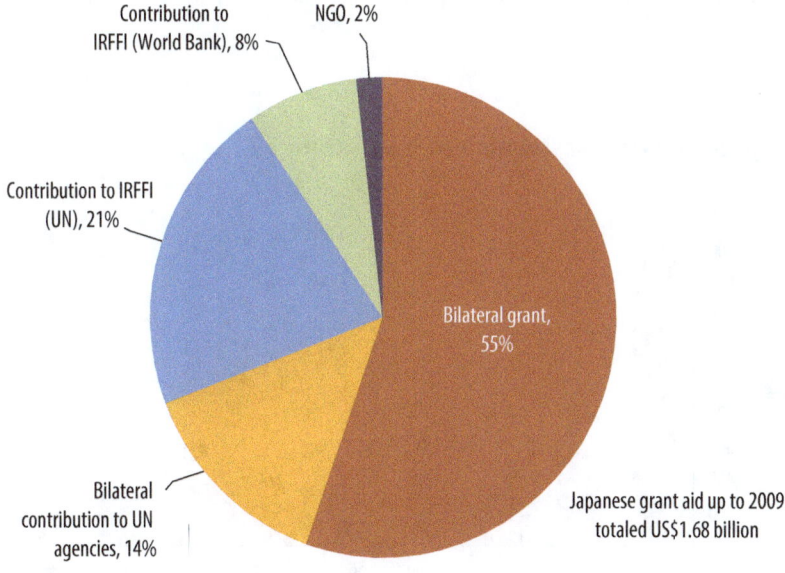

Source: Japan Ministry of Foreign Affairs 2009.
Note: IRFFI = International Reconstruction Fund Facility for Iraq; NGO = nongovernmental organization; UN = United Nations.

supervised jointly by the Japan Ministry of Finance and Ministry of Foreign Affairs and was executed by the Japan International Cooperation Agency (JICA) and the Japan Bank for International Cooperation (JBIC).[4]

Like the EU and United Kingdom, Japan provided aid to Iraq through multiple channels, but it also maintained large bilateral operations administered by JICA and the JBIC through grants initially and later through concessional loan assistance that continues today (see figures 2.5 and 2.6, respectively, for details on Japanese grant and loan assistance). Japan also forgave US$6.7 billion in credit to Iraq based on an agreement reached at the Paris Club in November 2004, at which donors agreed to reduce Iraqi public debt by 80 percent. By the end of 2016, Japan's total commitment for the reconstruction of Iraq had topped US$7 billion.

Evaluations of bilateral donor interventions are limited, so it is difficult to assess how aid affected the reconstruction of Iraq. However, the Iraq Inquiry Committee in the United Kingdom, led by John Chilcot, conducted a detailed assessment of the policies and actions of the United Kingdom in Iraq, including its reconstruction activities. The report contains key findings related to reconstruction:

- The committee stated that, from the available information, it was unable to assess the full impact of U.K. reconstruction efforts, noting, "One difficulty is that the [U.K.] government never defined what contribution reconstruction should make to achieving broader U.K. objectives and so what would constitute success or failure."

FIGURE 2.6

Japanese Loan Assistance to Iraq, 2006–13

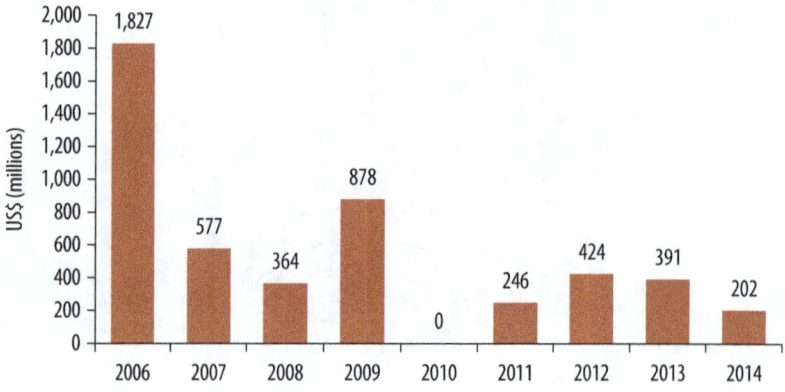

Source: Japan Ministry of Foreign Affairs database.
Note: US$1 = ¥100.

- The United Kingdom failed to plan or prepare for the major reconstruction program that would be required in Iraq. Many of the failures that affected planning and preparation before the invasion persisted throughout the postconflict period. They included poor interdepartmental coordination, inadequate civilian-military cooperation, and a failure to use resources coherently.

- An unstable and insecure environment made it increasingly difficult to make progress on reconstruction. Although staff and contractors developed innovative ways to deliver projects and manage risks, the constraints were never overcome.

- The U.K. cabinet agreed in July 2003 that the United Kingdom should make CPA South, a United Kingdom–led regional hub covering the southern governorates, a model for the reconstruction of Iraq, but the resources allocated to achieving this objective were insufficient to accomplish the task.

- Lessons learned through successive reviews of the U.K. approach to previous postconflict reconstruction and stabilization operations were not applied in Iraq after 2003.

The report of the Iraq Inquiry Committee was critical of many aspects of U.K. engagement, but it also demonstrated that the United Kingdom had a more inclusive approach and comprehensive view of the challenges to come in Iraq than its coalition partner, the United States. This point was reaffirmed through interviews with former U.S. reconstruction staff during the course of this study's research. While U.K. nationals temporarily assigned to the CPA were among those providing valuable advice to the United States–led occupation force, their recommendations had only a limited impact on the policies and overall course of early reconstruction efforts.[5]

United Nations and World Bank Activities in Iraq

In Iraq, both the UN and the World Bank found themselves facing challenges unlike any encountered in their previous postconflict engagements. For one thing, the status and legitimacy of the engagement of international organizations were unclear, particularly for the UN. In postwar situations, the UN performs diverse roles on multiple fronts, but it is most prominent in two areas: (1) humanitarian relief and reconstruction activities and (2) promotion of political transition and reconciliation. UNSC Resolution 1483 set out a basic framework for the governance and reconstruction of Iraq after the invasion. It vested the United Kingdom and the United States, as occupying forces, with executive, judicial, and legislative authority to be exercised through the CPA.

The resolution stated that the UN "should play a vital role in humanitarian relief, the reconstruction of Iraq, and the restoration and establishment of national and local institutions for representative governance" (UNSC 2003b, 1). Immediately after the invasion, the UN humanitarian agencies played a large role in extending emergency relief to vulnerable Iraqis affected by the war. As needs shifted to medium- to long-term reconstruction, the UN's role remained ambiguous (UNSC 2003a, 3). Moreover, some have questioned whether its mission received adequate support from the CPA on the ground.[6]

As for the World Bank and the International Monetary Fund, UNSC Resolution 1483 called on the international financial institutions "to assist the people of Iraq in the reconstruction and development of their economy and to facilitate assistance by the broader donor community" (UNSC 2003b, 4). Thus, the international financial institutions were expected to play a designated role in the financial and economic areas in which they hold expertise. Although the relationship was far from smooth, the CPA generally accepted some degree of advice from the international financial institutions in several economic policy areas, such as state-owned banks.

Like other actors, UN operations were subject to unprecedented security threats. An attack on August 19, 2003, that killed 22 officials—including the special representative of the UN secretary-general, Sergio Vieira de Mello—was only one in a series of attacks carried out against the UN and other international donors in the summer and fall of that year. As a result, the UN gradually reduced its presence within Iraq, removing most personnel by the end of 2003. It would be several years before the UN would return to full in-country operations.

Another challenge stemmed from the total lack of available data, such as fiscal information, economic statistics, and public service indicators. The IMF had not conducted a technical analysis of Iraq's economy for 20 years, and Iraqi data collection entities had atrophied under the Saddam regime (SIGIR 2009, 30). Without reliable data, efforts by the IMF and the World Bank were hobbled from the outset.

The preinvasion experiences of the UN and the World Bank in Iraq were quite different. Prior to the invasion, the UN and its agencies were present on the ground conducting the organization's standard country operations as well as administering elements of the Oil-for-Food Programme (OFFP) after 1995 (box 2.1). Unlike the UN, prior to 2003 the World Bank had not conducted any operations in Iraq for decades. From 1950 to 1973, the World Bank extended six International Bank for Reconstruction and Development (IBRD) loans to Iraq, with the last closing in 1979 (Iraq stopped making repayments in 1990) (Hadad-Zervos 2005).

> **BOX 2.1**
>
> **The Oil-for-Food Programme**
>
> Under economic sanctions imposed after the Gulf War in 1991, the OFFP was established to allow Iraq to sell oil on the world market in exchange for food, medicine, and other humanitarian needs for ordinary Iraqi citizens without boosting its military capabilities. The UN's role in administering the OFFP differed in central and southern Iraq, which fell under the rule of the Saddam regime, and in northern Iraq, which was governed by the Kurdistan Regional Government (KRG). The UN allocated 59 percent of oil revenue to the 15 central and southern governorates; 13 percent to the three northern governorates; 25 percent to a war reparations fund for victims of Iraq's invasion of Kuwait in 1990; and 3 percent to cover the UN's administrative costs, including those of the weapons inspectors. In the center and south, the UN, through the Office of the Iraq Program and the Security Council's Iraq Sanctions Committee, was responsible for overseeing the OFFP. In the north, the UN agencies were a de facto executing body for program delivery, along with regional government institutions. As a result, several UN agencies retained staff and consultants across the Kurdistan region. For example, UNDP, which was responsible for the Electricity Network Rehabilitation Program, had more than 80 international staff and engineers based in the north.
>
> The UN's engagement in OFFP had mixed consequences for the organization's postinvasion activities. On the one hand, it meant that the organization had developed knowledge, experience, and networks within Iraq. On the other hand, Iraqi public servants who had worked for the Saddam regime held mixed feelings toward UN intervention in their activities, illicit or otherwise. Furthermore, a scandal related to the OFFP that emerged later significantly damaged the image of the UN in Iraq.

It is difficult to calculate the size of the UN's financial engagement in reconstruction since its resources came from diverse sources, spending occurred through multiple agencies, and much data outside of the IRFFI, which served as a multidonor trust fund for Iraq's reconstruction, are not available.[7] The Iraq Ministry of Planning developed the Iraq Development Management System (IDMS) to identify donor activities;[8] however, the figures for UN agencies do not indicate the extent of cumulative UN spending in Iraq.[9]

The scale of the World Bank's financial engagement in Iraq is easier to measure, since most of its activities were disclosed systematically. The World Bank had several sources of funding for its reconstruction activities up to 2014: donor contributions to the IRFFI (US$494.4 million), concessional loans from its own International Development Association (US$500 million), IBRD loans (US$605 million),[10] and grant technical assistance sourced mainly from its own funds.

International Nongovernmental Organizations

The activities of international and national NGOs were highly constrained during the Saddam regime in all areas outside of the semiautonomous Kurdistan region. After the invasion in 2003, many international NGOs launched humanitarian operations inside Iraq. According to a report by the NGO Coordination Committee for Iraq (NCCI), a critical issue confronting many international NGOs at the beginning of their activities was their relationship with the occupation force, which was keen to draw on their support in the implementation of reconstruction activities. Given lingering questions over the legitimacy of the invasion, many international NGOs were afraid to be perceived as supporting a controversial war. They also knew that such support would enhance the risks to their staff. While some international NGOs kept their distance from the occupation force, some American international NGOs chose to work directly with the CPA and even used military escorts for their operations. For many Iraqis, who were not used to dealing with international NGOs, it was often difficult to distinguish between the roles of the international NGOs and contractors working for the CPA (Génot 2010, 16).

The NCCI was established in July 2003 in Baghdad to improve coordination among international NGOs and, later, with Iraqi national NGOs. In the beginning, the NCCI had 14 international NGO members; by the end of 2012, this number had climbed to 69: 37 international NGOs, 27 national NGOs, and 5 observers. The NCCI developed a useful platform for working in partnership and for exchanging information among NGOs undertaking operations in Iraq. But following the kidnapping and murder of some international NGO staff in late 2004, international NGOs eventually chose to remove staff from Iraq. As a result, many began to implement their assistance operations on a remote basis. In this context, partnerships with national NGOs in Iraq and other local groups took on added importance. The NCCI later looked back and realized that the departure of international NGOs from Iraq created an opportunity for Iraqi structures to emerge and develop, and this happened mostly out of necessity. By leaving Iraq, international NGOs made an unintended and indirect contribution to the birth of the Iraqi NGO sector (Génot 2010, 17).

Challenges to the International Response

Donor Coordination

Since multiple donors and other stakeholders are often engaged in reconstruction activities, the establishment of an effective coordination mechanism is critical. At the same time, the transaction costs of coordination need to be considered carefully. Four main coordination mechanisms were established in Iraq, encompassing multilateral and bilateral donors, Iraqi institutions, NGOs, and, in the early stage, the CPA:

- *The CPA's donor coordination mechanism.* CPA Regulation no. 7 of December 2003 created a framework for donor coordination, including bilateral and multilateral aid, and established the Iraq Strategic Review Board (ISRB). The ISRB—a committee comprising the Iraq minister of planning and development cooperation, the minister of finance, a representative of the CPA, and two ISRB secretariat members—served as a hub for coordinating donor activities, including loans, grants, guarantees, and technical assistance. While reconstruction programs required prior ISRB clearance to prevent duplication, the relevant sector ministries were charged with coordinating directly with donors and international organizations in the implementation of programs. The Council for International Coordination was set up to provide advice and support on coordination issues (figure 2.7; UN and World Bank 2003).

FIGURE 2.7

Donor Coordination Mechanism Led by Iraqi Entities

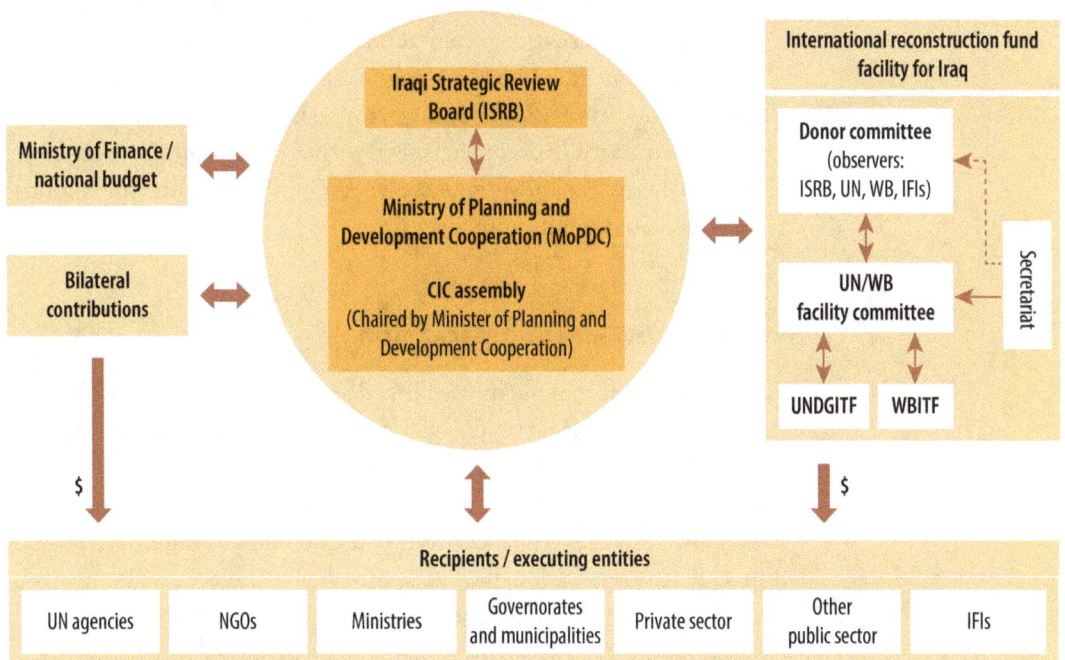

Source: UN and World Bank 2003.
Note: CIC = Council for International Coordination; UN = United Nations; WB = World Bank; IFI = international financial institution; UNDGITF = United Nations Development Group Iraq Trust Fund; WBITF = World Bank Iraq Trust Fund; NGO = nongovernmental organization.

- *Coordination for IRFFI.* IRFFI was structured into the coordination mechanism under the ISRB. To ensure coordination between IRFFI's two trust fund windows (the UN and World Bank), two committees—the Donor Committee and the UN–World Bank Facility Coordination Committee—were established. During the first four years, donor meetings were held regularly and frequently, but as international attention on Iraq's reconstruction receded, donor commitment to the IRFFI declined significantly and its coordination role among donors gradually weakened.

- *The United Nations–led cluster system.* In 2004, to ensure a comprehensive thematic approach, the United Nations Development Group (UNDG) introduced a new coordination mechanism, known as the cluster system. At the outset, thematic groups were established for 11 areas, but later merged into seven thematic areas. The system's main objective was to enhance coordination among UN agencies, and its function later expanded to include coordination with Iraqi institutions and other donors and actors. The system facilitated the distribution of resources among UN agencies from the UNDGITF.

- *The International Compact with Iraq.* In 2007, the Iraqi government introduced a new initiative called the International Compact with Iraq, in partnership with the UN and supported by the World Bank. The compact established benchmarks and mutual commitments for Iraq and the international community regarding normalizing the security environment, reconciling political divisions, and revitalizing economic conditions. This initiative marked the transition from a donor-led coordination mechanism to an Iraq-led mechanism. Here, as elsewhere, Iraqi government ownership of the reconstruction process increased significantly over time.

International Financing Mechanism

The international community established a trust fund called the IRFFI as an international mechanism for financing reconstruction activities in Iraq, raising a total of US$1.86 billion from diverse donors. According to the IRFFI's terms of reference, the fund's role was to ensure a coordinated, flexible, and swift donor response to finance priority expenditures, including reconstruction activities, sectorwide programs, investment projects, technical assistance, and other development activities (UN and World Bank 2003). Evaluations of IRFFI's effectiveness found the following:

- The IRFFI showed a high level of technical flexibility and stakeholder engagement during its initial phase, but weaknesses in the governance structure emerged early. Iraqi government engagement was limited, in particular under the UNDGITF. In addition, the frequency of Donor Committee meetings declined steadily between 2005 and 2007, when security conditions deteriorated. The Donor Committee did not provide adequate strategic guidance or oversight during that period.[11]

- With just one exception, the completion of most IRFFI projects was delayed, on average, 130 percent over the approved duration for UNDGITF projects and 70 percent for WBITF projects.

- By 2007, criticism of the IRFFI was widespread, particularly in relation to the UNDGITF portfolio.[12] Several factors contributed to this perception: (1) weaknesses in project-level reporting created a planning and credibility problem for the UNDGITF;[13] (2) the Steering Committee consisted of only participating UN agencies (an independent review has since raised questions about conflicts of interest, lack of independent oversight, and a culture that is too uncritical when assessing projects); and (3) interface with Iraqi institutions was limited.

- The full potential of IRFFI's two-window model could have been better realized had the World Bank and UN worked together more closely in programming jointly and in coordinating their activities (PwC 2011, 134). Interviews for this research with both former UN and World Bank staff suggest that coordination between the two institutions was better than reported, but that problems lay in differences between the two institutions' internal processing, policies on operations in insecure environments, and lack of a common secretariat.

The IRFFI experience showed that pooling resources through the establishment of a multidonor trust fund is important for realizing effective and swift reconstruction, while reducing the costs to each donor. However, compared with all of the efforts made by donors, UN agencies, and the World Bank, the size of the trust fund was relatively small in relation to the Iraqi capital investment budget. Between 2005 and 2010, Iraqi budget investment expenditures increased from ID 7,559 billion (US$5.2 billion) to ID 24,944 billion (US$25.6 billion; World Bank 2014, 33). Compared with the size of Iraqi investment budgets, the financial impact of the IRFFI was relatively small.

The Planning and Needs Assessment Process

In addition to the volatile political and security situation, effective reconstruction planning was made difficult by the scarcity of reliable data and the lack of recent experience, knowledge, and network contacts among actors prior to the invasion. Prewar planning and postwar assessment efforts undertaken for the reconstruction of Iraq faced many challenges.

Despite early criticism for a lack of proper preparation, information disclosed later showed that extensive U.S. planning took place ahead of the invasion. One of the most rigorous initiatives—the Future of Iraq project—was launched in early 2002 by the U.S. Department of State's Bureau of Near Eastern Affairs and tasked with studying postinvasion needs in Iraq, featuring analysis from several hundred Iraqi exiles and U.S.-based subject matter experts. Other parts of the U.S. government undertook their own prewar planning initiatives, including the National Security Council (Steering Executive Group on Iraq and the interagency Humanitarian Working Group), the U.S. Department of Defense (Energy Infrastructure Planning Group), and USAID (Iraq Task Force). However, these initiatives suffered from two problems: first, they were poorly coordinated with each other, and second, many of their recommendations were not adopted in the reconstruction activities that took place after the invasion.

According to interviews conducted for this research, some of the UN agencies did engage in planning exercises for postwar Iraq, but primarily for humanitarian needs. When the initial military operations of the invasion were drawing to a close, in June 2003, UN agencies and the World Bank, in consultation with the IMF, led a needs assessment process in 14 priority sectors. The needs assessment set out to define Iraq's reconstruction requirements and identify investment needs and priorities for the short and medium terms. But in the middle of the assessment process, the UN headquarters in Baghdad was attacked, leading many team members to be evacuated from the country. Nevertheless, the needs assessment process continued remotely with assistance from Iraqi national staff, and the findings were presented to the international community at the Madrid Donor Conference in October 2003.

Working with Iraqi Institutions

Each international actor engaged in reconstruction efforts in Iraq adopted a different approach to dealing with Iraqi counterparts and institutions, and many approaches changed over time.

Initially, the U.S. reconstruction team led by the CPA administered most reconstruction activities directly, with only limited involvement of Iraqi institutions. Before establishment of the CPA, the Office of Reconstruction and Humanitarian Assistance had endeavored to include Iraqi institutions in reconstruction, as they were seen as crucial to the swift establishment of an interim Iraqi authority. But with the issuance of CPA Order no. 1 on May 16, 2003, which established the CPA as the de facto government in Iraq, the efforts of ORHA and others to establish an interim Iraqi authority came to a halt.[14] Over time, U.S. reconstruction efforts became more inclusive, beginning with the return of sovereignty to the Iraqi transitional government in June 2004 and later during the U.S. military "surge" under the leadership of General David Petraeus and Ambassador Ryan Crocker.

For most project work, UN agencies adopted a flexible implementation modality, known as the direct execution (DEX) scheme, through which they were able to implement projects and programs directly. Under the DEX modality, agencies were able either to implement projects directly or to employ an implementing entity such as a private contractor or an NGO, with little engagement from Iraqi government institutions. Such a scheme has a certain merit in postconflict situations, where aid must be delivered quickly and counterpart national institutions are often weak. However, the lack of engagement by Iraqi institutions made such projects less sustainable and did little to contribute to institutional capacity development.

Compared with CPA and UN operations, the World Bank's implementation approach to projects fostered a significant degree of engagement by Iraqi government institutions. This was in large part due to the fact that the World Bank structured its operations based on its typical lending practices, which channel loans through partner countries for each project and program. In the case of Iraq's reconstruction, although initial funding came mainly via IRFFI grants and Iraqi institutional capacity was weak, the World Bank still chose to implement projects through Iraqi institutions, setting up project management teams composed of Iraqi government personnel from counterpart institutions who were put in charge of day-to-day implementation activities, interacting closely with World Bank project task managers.

This collaborative approach, however, resulted in significant delays in project implementation. These findings are elaborated upon in an independent review of 22 projects funded by the WBITF (GHK Consulting 2011, 9). Projects financed by the IRFFI fell into two broad groups. The first group of 11 projects focused on strengthening basic infrastructure to improve public services such as water, education, and health. Since most of these projects showed little progress two years after their initiation, in 2006 the Bank decided to change its project selection strategy. The second group was composed of smaller projects that many thought would be easier to manage, focusing primarily on institutional reforms and policy analyses. These projects supported various types of institutional strengthening in select ministries to improve budgeting, support banking reform, foster a more serious approach to environmental issues, and improve the efficiency of the electricity sector. Despite their smaller size, the second group of projects encountered the same difficulties as the first group and had even less impact on meeting the urgent needs of the Iraqi population.

Notes

1. This organizational complexity can be illustrated by the roles and relationships of the entities created to manage the reconstruction program. The CPA and the PMO were established to manage reconstruction projects conducted using U.S. resources. Both the CPA and the PMO reported to the U.S. Department of Defense. After sovereignty was transferred to the Iraqi interim government in June 2004, the CPA was dissolved, and most of its functions were transferred to the U.S. Embassy in Baghdad. The newly created IRMO took on a supervisory role for all reconstruction activities. Meanwhile, the PMO's project management role was transferred to the newly established PCO. Although IRMO was supposed to supervise the PCO, the PCO reported to the Department of Defense, while IRMO reported to the Department of State. In December 2005, the PCO was merged with USACE.
2. Dollar equivalents are calculated at £1 = US$1.74.
3. Dollar equivalents are calculated at €1 = US$1.31.
4. The official development assistance functions of the JBIC, including assistance to Iraq through concessional loans, were merged with JICA in October 2008.
5. Emma Sky, governorate coordinator for Kirkuk, and Rory Stewart, deputy governorate coordinator in several southern governorates, provided useful insights on this aspect in their publications (see Sky 2015; Stewart 2006).
6. Among others, Larry Diamond expressed this view in a 2004 *Foreign Affairs* article, "What Went Wrong in Iraq": "Even before the attack, however, Washington—and Bremer, in Baghdad—proved unwilling to surrender any significant measure of control to the UN. The CPA leadership did not see a real need for the UN mission" (Diamond 2004, 46).
7. More than 10 former or incumbent UN staff members and managers engaged in the reconstruction of Iraq were interviewed for this study, but no relevant financial data were available.
8. With the support of the EU, UNDP, the UN Office for Project Services, USAID, and a few other donors, the Iraq Ministry of Planning developed the IDMS, which was designed to detail donor activities. However, the financial figures for UN agencies capture only part of their activities.
9. Information in the IDMS database was compared with information made available online by UN agencies.
10. The World Bank made new pledges totaling US$1.55 billion in 2015.
11. PwC (2011, 48) noted, "The active involvement of donors in the process of project review and approval proved important to ensuring transparency and preventing conflicts of interest."
12. Scanteam (2009, 61) noted, "The lack of a central body responsible for oversight and evaluation of results of all projects under the Trust Fund raised a number of issues. ... Each agency was indeed responsible for monitoring and

evaluating its own projects and the Steering Committee did not have a mandate to oversee or monitor ongoing projects funded by the UNDG ITF."
13. The UN disclosed most information concerning funded projects and programs, so criticism of its reporting practices may not be justified.
14. SIGIR (2009, 71) noted, "The postwar strategy for Iraq approved by the President on March 10, 2003 assumed that the country's governing institutions would survive the invasion and remain sufficiently intact to continue to administer the offices of government and provide the Iraqi people with the essential services. The new regulation signaled a developing shift in U.S. policy."

References

Diamond, Larry. 2004. "What Went Wrong in Iraq." *Foreign Affairs* 83 (5): 34–56.

EU (European Union). 2010. *Cooperation between the European Union and Iraq: Joint Strategy Paper 2011–2013.* Brussels: EU.

Génot, Cécile. 2010. *International NGOs in Iraq: Actors or Witnesses in the Evolution of the Iraqi NGO Sector?* Draft report. Baghdad: NGO Coordination Committee for Iraq. https://www.alnap.org/system/files/content/resource/files/main/ncci-survey-ingos-iraqi-ngos-draft-2.pdf.

GHK Consulting. 2011. *Independent Review of the Iraq Trust Fund World Bank: Final Report.* London: GHK Consulting.

Hadad-Zervos, Faris. 2005. *The World Bank in Iraq: Iraqi Ownership for Sustainability.* Washington, DC: World Bank.

International Development Committee, House of Commons. 2005. *Development Assistance in Iraq: Interim Report Seventh Report of Session 2004–05.* London: Stationery Office Limited.

Japan Ministry of Foreign Affairs. 2009. "Japan's Assistance to Iraq." Ministry of Foreign Affairs, Tokyo, August.

PwC (PricewaterhouseCoopers). 2011. *United Nations Development Group Iraq Trust Fund Lessons Learned Exercise.* New York: PwC. https://reliefweb.int/sites/reliefweb.int/files/resources/UNDGITF_LL_Report_EN.pdf.

Scanteam. 2009. *Stocktaking Review of the International Reconstruction Fund Facility for Iraq Final Report.* Oslo: Scanteam Analysts and Advisers.

SIGIR (Special Inspector General for Iraq Reconstruction). 2009. *Hard Lessons: The Iraq Reconstruction Experience.* Washington, DC: U.S. Government Printing Office.

———. 2013. *Learning from Iraq: A Final Report from the Special Inspector General for Iraq Reconstruction.* Washington, DC: SIGIR. https://www.globalsecurity.org/military/library/report/2013/sigir-learning-from-iraq.pdf.

Sky, Emma. 2015. *The Unraveling: High Hopes and Missed Opportunities in Iraq.* New York: Public Affairs.

Stewart, Roy. 2006. *The Prince of the Marshes: And Other Occupational Hazards of a Year in Iraq.* New York: Harcourt.

Tarnoff, Curt. 2009. *Iraq Reconstruction Assistance*. Washington, DC: Congressional Research Service.

UN (United Nations) and World Bank. 2003. "International Reconstruction Fund Facility for Iraq, Terms of Reference." Unpublished document, World Bank, Washington, DC, December. http://siteresources.worldbank.org/IRFFI/Resources/RevisedTORS.pdf.

UNSC (UN Security Council). 2003a. *Report of the Secretary General Pursuant to Paragraph 24 of Resolution 1483 (2003) and Paragraph 12 of Resolution 1511 (2003)*. New York: United Nations. https://documents-dds-ny.un.org/doc/UNDOC/GEN/N04/449/31/PDF/N0444931.pdf?OpenElement.

———. 2003b. "United Nations Security Council Resolution (UNSCR) 1483." United Nations, New York, May. http://unscr.com/en/resolutions/doc/1483.

U.S. GAO (Government Accountability Office). 2004. *Rebuilding Iraq: Resource, Security, Governance, Essential Services, and Oversight Issues*. Washington, DC: GAO. https://www.gao.gov/products/GAO-04-902R.

World Bank. 2014. *Republic of Iraq Public Expenditure Review*. Washington, DC: World Bank.

CHAPTER 3

The Reconstruction of Iraqi Infrastructure and Human Capital

When reconstruction activities began, donors and international organizations had not reached a consensus on what they were trying to achieve. Many donors were concerned only with those activities aimed at restoring economic and social infrastructure and allocated the bulk of their available resources to these priorities. Through the course of this research, many Iraqi interviewees said that the impact of reconstruction remains disappointingly inconspicuous considering the amount of money spent. While repeated insurgent attacks on infrastructure were a major hindrance to the recovery, other factors were to blame as well, including the excessively supply-driven nature of donor efforts, a lack of engagement with and from Iraqi institutions, and insufficient or ineffective efforts to build institutional capacity. This chapter assesses recovery efforts for the electricity, oil, education, and health sectors.

The Electricity Sector

A chronic shortage of electricity continues to make life difficult for the Iraqi public and the Iraqi economy. Temperatures can rise to as much as 50°C during the summer months, and on several occasions since 2003, the lack of power coupled with high temperatures have led to popular protests, sometimes violent ones, to demand better service. Unstable supply and frequent outages have also lowered production and damaged capital assets. The problem has been especially acute in the oil sector, where plants and refineries rely on electricity to power equipment and to transport oil, which, in turn, affects power generation plants reliant on a steady supply of fuel.

FIGURE 3.1

Electricity Generation Capacity in Iraq, 2002–14

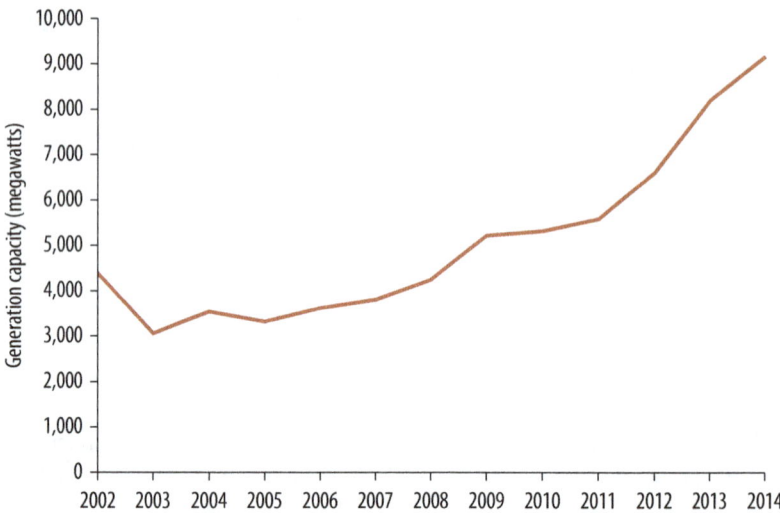

Source: Iraq Ministry of Electricity data.

After the invasion in 2003, Iraq's electricity-generating capacity dropped to 3,300 megawatts from its prewar level of 4,400 megawatts (figure 3.1).[1] There was only limited damage to the country's electricity infrastructure during the invasion, but subsequent looting damaged many facilities. The headquarters of the Commission of Electricity (which was later upgraded to ministry status) was sacked and set alight, destroying information and data and requiring staff to relocate to the better-protected Ministry of Oil building.

United States–Led Reconstruction in the Electricity Sector, 2003–05

While the United States was not the only donor to provide assistance to the electricity sector, its financial contribution was far greater than that of other donors, and U.S. agencies played far bigger roles in the sector's reconstruction, particularly during the first several years. The Coalition Provisional Authority (CPA) considered reconstruction of the electricity sector to be critical for reviving Iraq's economy, improving daily well-being, and gaining local support for the coalition's presence in Iraq, setting a goal of achieving 4,400 megawatts of generation capacity by October 2003 and 6,000 megawatts by June 30, 2004 (U.S. GAO 2007). This target was considered highly ambitious and unrealistic by those who knew the electricity sector and the condition of the facilities in Iraq; as it was, it took almost eight years to reach that level.

Outside of reaching its prewar generating capacity, Iraq's electricity sector saw little improvement in the first three years of reconstruction. United States–led efforts encountered several significant challenges:

- With little prewar planning conducted for the electricity sector, postwar efforts had to be undertaken with incomplete information.[2]

- To achieve the CPA's targets, many generating plants were forced into operation after receiving only basic emergency repairs and soon went out of service due to the strain on operations during the peak period in the summer of 2004. As a result, the subsequent year's capacity dropped (figure 3.2).

- To increase generating capacity rapidly, gas turbines, which require less installation time, were purchased. Due to the lack of natural gas as a fuel, however, many sat idle (SIGAR 2009, 148–50). Coordination with the oil sector team was not effective, compounding fuel shortages that consistently caused generation bottlenecks. Just as many of the gas turbines purchased could not operate due to a lack of gas, many oil facilities could not operate due to a lack of electricity, even as large amounts of gas from oil fields were flared and wasted.

FIGURE 3.2

Electricity Generation in Iraq, Average for May 2003 to December 2005

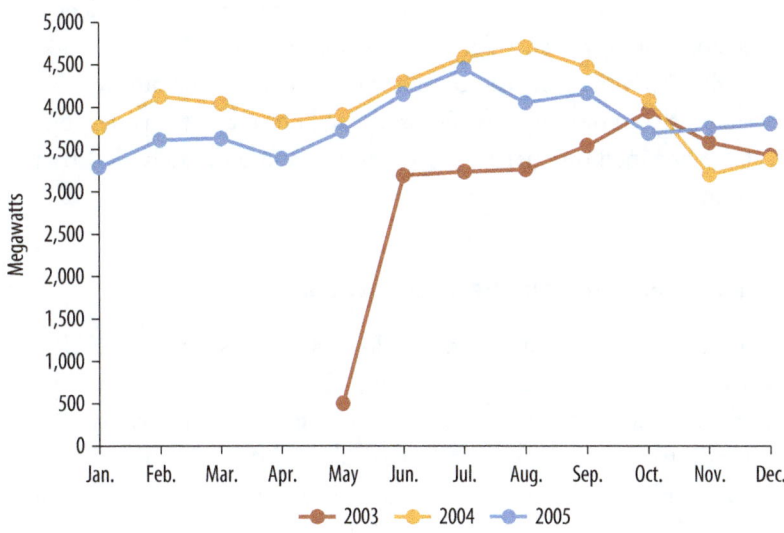

Source: O'Hanlon and Campbell 2007.

- The electricity sector was subject to budget reductions and frequent changes in priorities. Some US$5.5 billion was initially allocated to the sector, but as a result of reallocations to cover urgently needed spending on security, its budget was cut by US$1 billion.

- The organizational complexities of the electricity sector were made still more difficult after the CPA was dissolved and its functions were transferred to multiple agencies. The presence of two separate reporting lines—one to the U.S. Department of State and the other to the U.S. Department of Defense—complicated matters further.

- The U.S. advisers assigned to the electricity sector lacked experience in postwar reconstruction and work overseas. The U.K. Report of the Iraq Inquiry points out that the CPA's electricity team was small—just eight people, only three of whom were specialists—and was poorly managed (Williams Lea Group 2016, 111). In addition, turnover was very high, with senior advisers being replaced every three to four months during the first year (SIGIR 2009, 82–83).

- U.S. companies were awarded most of the available reconstruction contracts. For bilateral grant aid, many donors award contracts to their own national companies, but since this practice was also applied to the Development Fund for Iraq (DFI), which comprised Iraqi assets and oil revenues, the public perception grew in Iraq that the United States–led coalition was using Iraqi resources to enrich U.S. companies.

- U.S. officials installed their own choice of minister for the electricity sector, opting for an Iraqi exile previously engaged in anti–Saddam regime activities from the United States. This move created much tension with senior ministry officials in Iraq. The minister in question was later detained on charges of corruption and ultimately fled Iraq to return to the United States.

Other Donor Efforts in the Electricity Sector

In addition to the United States, donors such as Japan, the United Nations Development Programme (UNDP), and the World Bank engaged in several reconstruction projects in the electricity sector. Immediately following the invasion in 2003, UNDP and the World Bank took the lead in assessing the state of the sector. Under the Oil-for-Food Programme (OFFP), UNDP was responsible for the Electricity Network Rehabilitation Program in the north, retaining more than 80 international staff and engineers to execute and supervise electricity projects funded by OFFP. In addition, as a UN observer, several engineers were stationed in Baghdad to monitor the regime's activities in the electricity sector. UNDP implemented several electricity projects amounting to US$135 million, mainly from International Reconstruction Fund Facility for Iraq (IRFFI) funds and most of which involved the provision of spare parts and equipment, along with emergency repairs to gas turbine and thermal plants. Despite its experience during the years prior to 2003, UNDP engagement in the electricity sector was limited, and its interventions were fragmented.

The World Bank implemented one project to rehabilitate two generation units of a thermal power plant, funded by US$124 million from its concessional window and US$6 million from IRFFI. An evaluation compiled later rated this project's outcome as unsatisfactory because it failed to rehabilitate the plant fully.

Japan was another major donor active in the electricity sector, providing assistance to several electricity projects aimed at rehabilitating generation units and power grids as well as constructing new power units through bilateral grant aid amounting to US$380 million and concessional loans of US$1.5 billion. For other power generation units in the same power plant—the Hartha plant in Basra, which the World Bank failed to complete—Japan brought in a Japanese contractor and completed the rehabilitation work successfully. Today, Japan continues to provide assistance through concessional loans, so while some projects have been completed, others are still being implemented.

Improvements in Electricity Service

Despite some recovery in generating capacity and infrastructure, demand continued to outstrip supply, and the Integrated National Energy Strategy in 2012 estimated that approximately 42 percent of dispatched energy disappeared through technical losses, theft, or service for which payment was never collected (PMAC 2012). Many frustrated households and communities ended up installing individual diesel generators, which were loud, dirty, and generally expensive to operate.

One of the significant initiatives undertaken by Iraq's Ministry of Electricity was an agreement with private companies—Siemens of Germany and General Electric of the United States—to purchase more than US$7 billion worth of generators. Due to the lack of budget resources, not all of the planned projects involving the use of these generators were implemented. However, the provision of substantial numbers of generation units did, to some extent, improve Iraq's chronic power shortage.

The reconstruction of the electricity sector saw significant regional variance, particularly between the central and southern parts of Iraq and the Kurdistan region. During the Saddam regime, after the Gulf War in 1991 and subsequent Kurdish uprisings, the Kurdistan region was cut off from all national grid transmission lines, except for one near Mosul. Available generation for the region was limited mostly to supply from a few hydroelectric power stations. Other regions suffered too, with supply to the Baghdad region prioritized over supply to the rest of the country.

After the invasion, the situation changed drastically. The Kurdistan Regional Government (KRG) established its own Ministry of Electricity, and reconstruction work was undertaken by the KRG and central government ministries largely independent of each other. Despite the Kurdistan region's poor electricity infrastructure, its relatively greater stability meant that northern Iraq was soon enjoying a more reliable electricity supply than the center and south of the country (figure 3.3). The stark difference in customer satisfaction between regions demonstrates just how pronounced the differences in supply levels were (figure 3.4).

FIGURE 3.3

Electricity Supply from the National Grid in Iraq, 2007, 2011, and 2012

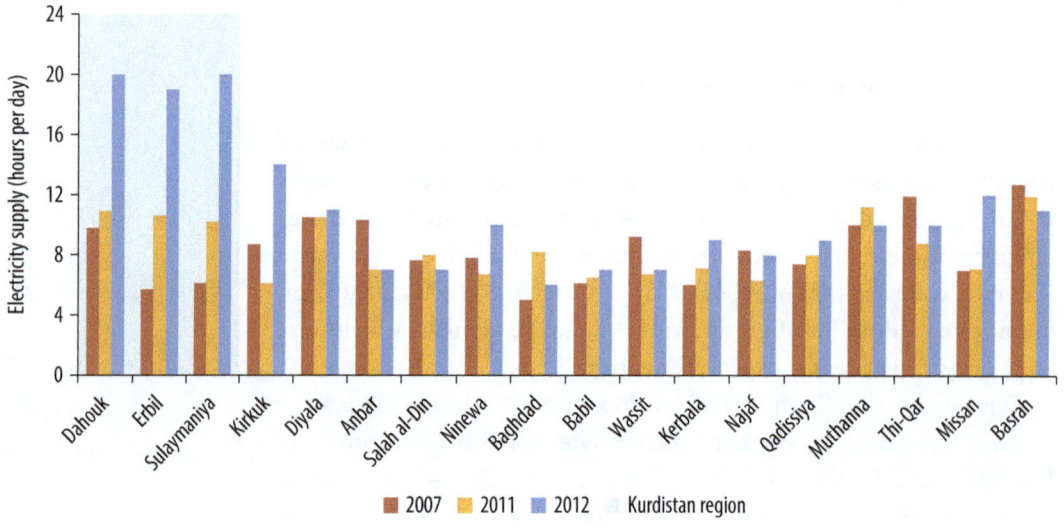

Sources: CSO, KRSO, and United Nations 2011; CSO, KRSO, and World Bank 2007, 2011.

FIGURE 3.4

Public Perceptions of Electricity Service Provision in Iraq, by Governorate, 2011

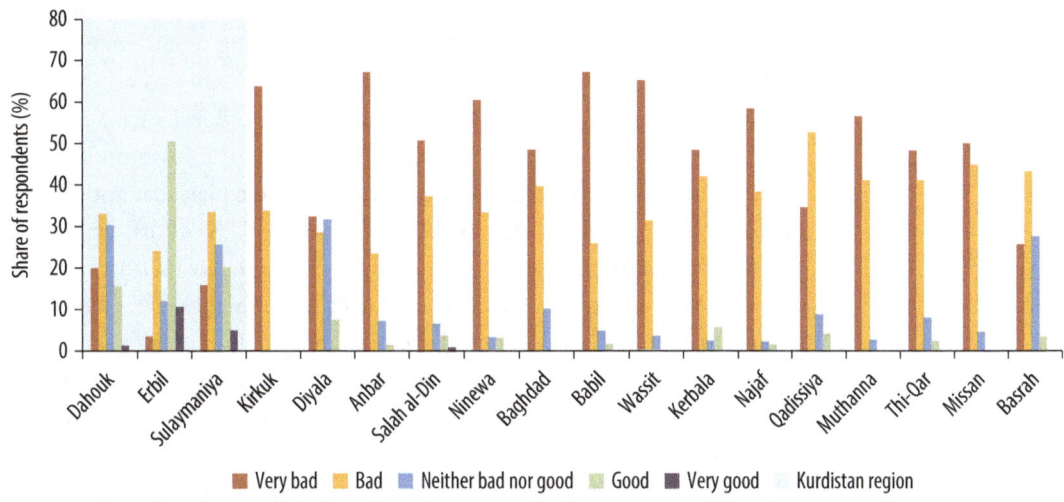

Source: CSO, KRSO, and World Bank 2011.

The Oil Sector

The presence of huge oil reserves in Iraq—some 115 billion barrels of known reserves, the world's fifth largest—motivated many donors as well as foreign private companies to engage in the reconstruction process.

United States–Led Reconstruction in the Oil Sector, 2003–05

Like the electricity sector, the United States played a leading role in reconstruction activities in Iraq's oil sector, and, unlike other sectors, donor engagement from elsewhere was limited.[3] Identified as a priority sector in prewar planning, the U.S. Department of Defense and the U.S. Department of State each set up task forces to study Iraq's existing capacity, as well as likely future needs and challenges. The Energy Infrastructure Planning Group (EIPG) was established under the Department of Defense in November 2002. A major prewar planning concern for EIPG and the U.S. Army Corps of Engineers (USACE) Task Force Restore Iraqi Oil centered on how to stop oil well fires in the event the Saddam regime set wells alight, as they had set fire to 700 wells during the first Gulf War. As it happened, no serious sabotage of the northern or southern oil fields occurred during the invasion, with only seven fires recorded (Vogler 2015).[4] However, considerable damage was inflicted by widespread looting as the occupation got under way. According to a subsequent USACE survey of Iraq's oil infrastructure, combat operations and the looting that followed caused US$1.4 billion in damage: US$457 million from military action and US$943 million from postwar looting. The report estimated reconstruction funding requirements to be US$1.7 billion (SIGIR 2009, 60).[5]

Crude oil production dropped from its prewar level of 2.5 million barrels per day to almost zero immediately after the invasion. In July 2003, Iraq's Ministry of Oil and the CPA initiated a plan that anticipated executing 226 projects costing US$1.14 billion. U.S. efforts in the oil sector focused largely on (1) restoring Iraq's oil infrastructure to prewar production and export capacity; (2) delivering refined fuels for domestic consumption; (3) developing oil security and pipeline repair teams; and (4) providing technical assistance to sustain Iraq's oil industry (U.S. GAO 2005). U.S. officials set a production goal of 3 million barrels of oil per day and an export goal of 2.2 million barrels of crude oil per day by the end of 2004. Crude oil production recovered relatively quickly, but production levels again dropped in mid-2004 as insurgent attacks on oil facilities intensified (figure 3.5; U.S. GAO 2007).

The oil sector's institutional environment in the wake of the invasion differed from that of other sectors in Iraq. First, the U.S. Office of Reconstruction and Humanitarian Assistance (ORHA) and, later, the CPA assigned experienced U.S. experts as sector advisers, many of whom had engaged in prewar planning exercises and continued to

FIGURE 3.5

Monthly Oil Production in Iraq, 2003–05

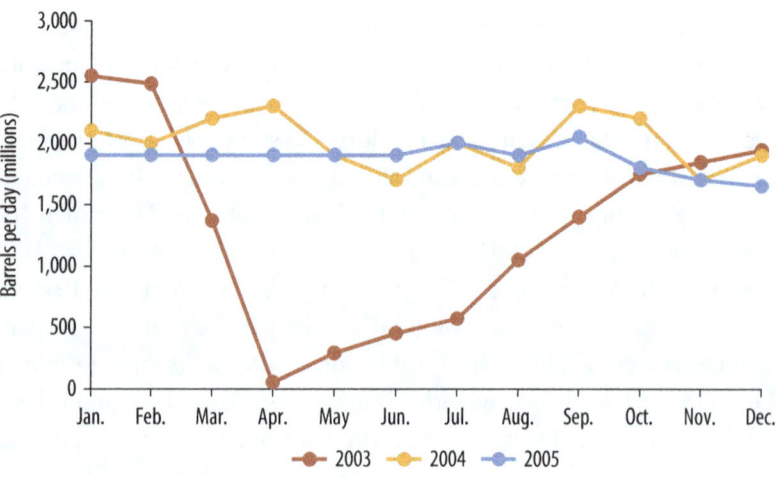

Source: O'Hanlon and Campbell 2008.

serve in Iraq after the invasion, ensuring continuity among advisers. Second, despite having suffered under economic sanctions during the 1990s and as a result of post-2003 de-Baathification, Iraq's Ministry of Oil had historically attracted the best and brightest Iraqi employees, and it retained greater capacity than other ministries. Together, the presence of experienced and committed U.S. experts and Iraqi ministry officials created an atmosphere of collaboration not seen in other sectors.

The United States allocated substantial budget resources to the sector, as indicated in table 3.1. In addition to the U.S. budget, by the end of 2005, a further US$2.8 billion had been spent out of the DFI.

Nevertheless, after its initial recovery, crude oil production showed little improvement in the first several years following the invasion (figure 3.5), with the sector encountering some significant difficulties:

- Continuous and intensifying insurgent attacks on oil facilities, in particular, on oil pipelines. Between 2003 and 2007, more than 400 attacks hit Iraq's pipelines, refineries, and workers (SIGIR 2013). The United States–led occupation force did not have enough troops to guard long oil pipelines and numerous oil facilities. As a result, the Ministry of Oil formed its own security force to protect these facilities.

- The need to mitigate the shortage of oil products, especially gasoline, became a significant preoccupation for officials and limited their ability to address other urgent needs.

- Key institutional reforms introduced by the CPA failed. In particular, despite resistance from ministry employees, the CPA insisted on persevering with the dysfunctional payroll system it had introduced after the invasion (Vogler 2015).

- The governing council's decision to appoint an inexperienced Iraqi exile without leadership skills as oil minister in September 2003 hurt ministry operations (Vogler 2015).

TABLE 3.1

U.S. Budget Allocations for the Iraqi Oil Sector, as of September 30, 2006

		Funding (US$, millions)	
Source of funds	Agency	Budgeted	Spent
2003 Iraq Relief and Reconstruction Fund (IRRF I)	U.S. Department of Defense	166.0	166.0
Natural Resource Risk Remediation Fund	U.S. Department of Defense	802.0	797.7
2004 Iraq Relief and Reconstruction Fund (IRRF II)	U.S. Department of Defense	1,724.7	1,163.0
Total		2,692.7	2,126.7

Source: SIGIR 2009.

Private Sector Involvement in Restoring Oil Production

The United States completed the majority of its planned oil sector projects by mid-2007, at which point the government of Iraq began to take on still greater ownership of oil and natural gas sector reconstruction, introducing several policy initiatives that included the drafting of federal hydrocarbon laws and the completion of a round of oil field auctions started in 2008. To date, the hydrocarbon laws have yet to be approved officially due to disagreement on control and decision-making authority in the hydrocarbon sector, most notably the question of revenue sharing between the center and the regions (IEA 2012).

After a long period of limited growth, crude oil production finally started to rise steadily after the oil fields developed by international oil companies went into production in 2010 (figure 3.6). The government of Iraq led several rounds of oil field auctions, with assistance from the consulting firm Gaffney, Cline & Associates; to date, the federal government has awarded 19 technical service contracts (table 3.2). Greater Iraqi institutional ownership and private sector participation laid the foundations for further sector recovery.

FIGURE 3.6

Crude Oil Production in Iraq before and after International Oil Company Engagement, 2003–15

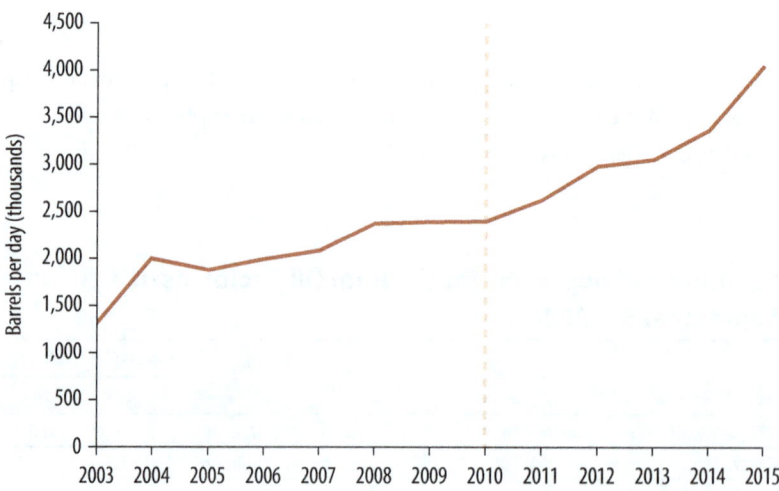

Source: U.S. Energy Information Administration 2016.

TABLE 3.2

Contracts Awarded by Federal Authorities for Hydrocarbon Exploration and Development in Iraq

Year and bid round	Project or block	Operator	Type	Production (barrels per day for oil; cubic meters, billions, for gas)		Maximum fee per barrel (US$)[c]
				Initial target[a]	Plateau target[b]	
2008	Ahdab	Petrochina	Oil	25,000	129,000	6.00
2009 First	Rumaila	BP	Oil	1,173,000	2,850,000	2.00
	West Qurna I	ExxonMobil	Oil	268,000	2,825,000	1.90
	Zubair	Eni	Oil	201,000	1,200,000	2.00
	Missan Group	CNOOC	Oil	97,000	450,000	2.30
2009 Second	West Qurna II	Lukoil	Oil	120,000	1,800,000	1.15
	Majnoon	Shell	Oil	175,000	1,800,000	1.39
	Halfaya	Petrochina	Oil	70,000	535,000	1.40
	Gharraf	Petronas	Oil	35,000	230,000	1.49
	Badra	GazpromNeft	Oil	15,000	170,000	5.50
	Qairayah	Sonangol	Heavy oil	30,000	120,000	5.00
	Najmah	Sonangol	Heavy oil	20,000	110,000	6.00
2010	Akkas	KOGAS	Gas	1.03	4.1	5.50
	Mansuriyah	TPAO	Gas	0.78	3.1	7.00
	Siba	Kuwait Energy	Gas	0.26	1.0	7.50
2012	Block 8	Pakistan Petroleum	Gas	n.a.	n.a.	5.38
	Block 9	Kuwait Energy	Oil	n.a.	n.a.	6.24
	Block 10	Lukoil	Oil	n.a.	n.a.	5.99
	Block 12	Bashneft	Oil	n.a.	n.a.	5.00

Source: IEA 2012.
Note: n.a. = not applicable (no targets set).
a. Level of production at which contractors can start receiving cost reimbursements and the payment of fees.
b. Maximum level of production that contractors agreed to deliver.
c. Maximum remuneration per barrel that contractors can receive.

The Education Sector

Between the 1970s and the mid-1980s, Iraq was considered to have the best education system in the region. The government at the time had a clear policy priority—to enhance the quality of education in Iraq—and pursued many reforms during the 1970s. These reforms included the establishment of mandatory education at the primary level and free education at all levels; an increase in the number of universities; the introduction of free school meals in preschool and elementary school; increases in the number of scholarships to study abroad; and increases in teacher salaries. It was the golden age of the Iraqi education system (Yamao and Sakai 2013, 154).

This golden age did not last long. The war between the Islamic Republic of Iran and Iraq that raged from 1980 to 1988, the Gulf War in 1991, and ensuing economic sanctions all severely damaged the once-excellent education system. By the time the Iraq War started in 2003, the quality of the education system had dropped significantly. The system's deterioration coincided with shrinking budget allocations to the education sector. In fiscal year 1988/89, the education budget was US$2.5 billion (about 6 percent of gross domestic product [GDP]), and the expenditure per student was approximately US$620. Over the 1993–2002 period, the annual average expenditure per student dropped to approximately US$47, funded largely from the OFFP (Waite 2003, 14). As a result, school infrastructure broke down, as maintenance and new construction were deferred year after year. Teacher training, curricular modernization, monitoring and assessment, and the introduction of new teaching techniques became increasingly rare (World Bank 2011, 52).

According to the UN–World Bank joint needs assessment in 2003, while overall damage to school facilities from the invasion in 2003 was limited—only 79 schools were destroyed—the damage caused by subsequent looting was more serious (UN and World Bank 2003). Approximately 922 schools were looted in Anbar, Baghdad, Ninewah, Sala Heldin, and Tamim governorates.

Donor Support for the Education Sector

After 2003, the Iraqi government, with the support of donors and international organizations, committed to restoring the country's education system. Unlike other areas of infrastructure, the United States asserted far less control over reconstruction of the education sector in spite of its large financial contribution. As of September 2012, the U.S. government had spent US$379.4 million on rebuilding Iraq's school infrastructure and curriculum, three-fourths of which were used under the Commander's Emergency Response Program (SIGIR 2013, 113). The U.S. Agency for International Development (USAID) also played a major role in U.S. efforts in the education sector, providing more than 500,000 school kits and supporting school rehabilitation. By early 2006, USAID had supported the construction or improvement of 2,943 schools across the country (SIGIR 2013).

According to the United Nations Development Group Iraq Trust Fund (UNDGITF) database, UN agencies—mainly the United Nations Children's Fund (UNICEF); United Nations Educational, Scientific, and Cultural Organization (UNESCO); and UN-Habitat—spent approximately US$206 million across more than 30 projects. UNICEF and UNESCO also mobilized additional resources bilaterally from several donors—including the European Union, Japan, and the United States—and implemented several education projects. The World Bank implemented various education projects, including emergency textbook provision (US$38.8 million from IRFFI), emergency school construction and rehabilitation (US$55.2 million from IRFFI), and a separate emergency school reconstruction effort (US$100 million from the International Development Agency).

Overall, donor assistance in the education sectors was limited in scale and simple in scope: the provision of school supplies, the rehabilitation or construction of schools, revisions to the curriculum, and capacity development for teachers. While data are outdated and scarce, public spending on education stood at 3.5 percent of GDP in 2008, which is relatively low when compared with the spending of neighboring countries such as the Arab Republic of Egypt, Jordan, and Morocco, where spending amounted to approximately 6.3 percent of GDP (Supervisory Committee for National Strategy for Education and Higher Education 2012). Iraqi spending in the sector appears to have increased significantly in recent years, although the bulk of expenditures has gone to staff remuneration, leaving little for quality-related inputs such as teacher training and curriculum modernization. Between 2007 and 2009, the average cost of an education worker almost tripled. Between 2005 and 2008, the Ministry of Education experienced a 64 percent increase in staff and a 156 percent increase in the cost of compensating its employees; employee compensation doubled again a year later (World Bank 2017b, 78). Thus, the majority of the education budget went to recurrent budget expenses as opposed to capital expenditures (table 3.3).

Changes in Education Service Provision after 2003

The education sector has improved in recent years, but the available data are inconsistent, and the full picture remains unclear. The Ministry of Education's statistics show significant advances: the number of students enrolled in all stages of education in the academic year 2012–13 reached

TABLE 3.3

Types of Expenditures in the Education Budget in Iraq, 2005–11

Percent of total budget

Types of Expenditures	2005	2006	2007	2008	2009	2010	2011
Recurrent							
Original budget	4.2	4.2	5.4	5.4	9.5	8.8	8.6
Estimated actual	—	—	0.1	8.1	13.7	—	—
Capital							
Original budget	0.5	0.2	1.3	0.6	0.7	1.0	1.1
Estimated actual	0.1	0.0	—	1.0	0.7	—	—

Source: World Bank 2017a.
Note: — = not available.

FIGURE 3.7

Student Enrollment in Iraq, 2005–13

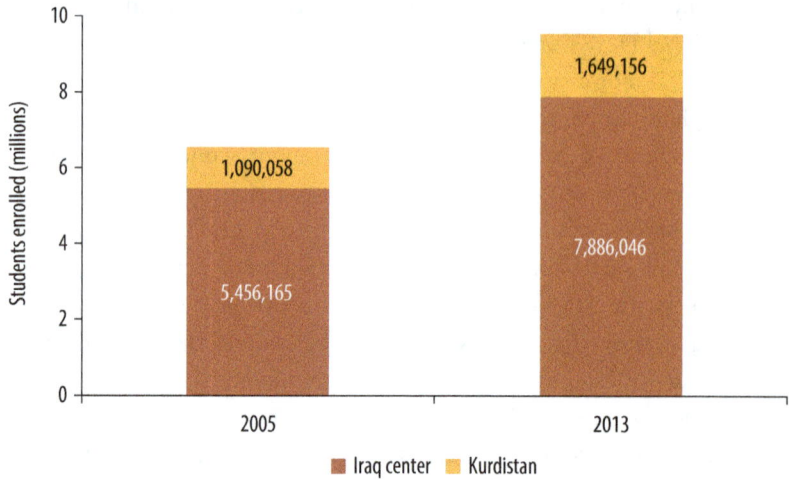

Source: Iraq Ministry of Education, quoted in UNICEF 2014.

9.5 million, up from 6.5 million in 2004–05; the number of schools increased to 28,730 in 2012–13, up from 20,508 in 2004; and over the same period, the number of instructors increased from 343,614 to 550,000 (figure 3.7; UNICEF 2014, 14–15).

According to data collected by UNICEF and the Iraqi government, the rate of enrollment in primary school increased from 76.3 percent in 2000 to 85.8 percent in 2006 and to 90 percent in 2011. While primary school enrollment improved significantly, secondary school enrollment struggled, increasing only modestly from 40.1 percent in 2006 to 48.6 percent in 2011. In general, the Kurdistan region fared better: primary school enrollment rose from 94.5 percent in 2006 to 95.9 percent in 2011, while secondary school enrollment jumped from 52.5 percent in 2006 to 71.9 percent in 2011. The stronger growth in secondary school enrollment in northern Iraq has been due in part to the KRG policy that makes grades 7–9 part of each student's compulsory basic education. Under the system run by the central government, education is compulsory only in grades 1–6 (table 3.4). The government has begun to increase the education budget, raising it from 5.3 percent of government spending in 2006 to 15 percent in 2009, much of which has gone to increasing teacher salaries (World Bank 2017b, 79). But the share of nonsalary expenditures remains low, and inadequate teacher training, poor instructional materials, and outdated curriculum continue to affect the quality of education in Iraq.

TABLE 3.4

Structure and Organization of Education in Iraq

Level of education	Organization
Iraq (excluding KRG)	
Preprimary education	Official entry age 4, 2 years, noncompulsory
Primary education (grades 1–6)	Official entry age 6, grades 1–6, compulsory, free of charge
Secondary education (grades 7–12)	Official entry age 12
Upper secondary or vocational	Theoretical entry age 15, 3 years
University and higher	4–5 years
KRG	
Preprimary education	Official entry age 4, 2 years, noncompulsory
Basic education	Official entry age 6, grades 1–9, compulsory, free of charge
Upper secondary education	Theoretical entry age 15, 3 years, noncompulsory
University and higher education	4–5 years

Source: UNESCO 2011, 24.
Note: KRG = Kurdistan Regional Government.

The Health Sector

In the early 1980s, Iraq had a reasonably well-performing health system able to provide basic and some high-level services to the vast majority of the population. However, years of war and economic sanctions in the ensuing decades hit the health system hard. Physical infrastructure such as hospitals and medical equipment suffered from a lack of proper maintenance, the unavailability of spare parts and equipment, and continuous underinvestment. The system's decline can be seen in the rising infant mortality rate between 1980 to 2001 and stagnant life expectancy numbers compared with the rest of the Middle East and North Africa region (figure 3.8; World Bank, various years).

Donor Support for the Health Sector

Since the fall of the Saddam regime, the Iraqi government, donors, and international organizations have expended a great deal of resources and energy on restoring the health system; however, the process has been slow and, although some health indicators have improved, change has been modest. For example, infant mortality improved some, dropping from 34.3 per 1,000 in 2003 to 28.2 per 1,000 in 2013, respectively (World Bank, various years). But the average life expectancy for Iraqis deteriorated slightly from 68.94 in 2002, right before the invasion, to 68.22 in 2008, while life expectancy in most Middle East and North African countries improved steadily.

The United States was a major actor in the reconstruction of Iraq's health sector, primarily through the work of USACE and USAID.

FIGURE 3.8

Infant Mortality Rate versus Life Expectancy at Birth in the Middle East and North Africa, 1980 and 2001

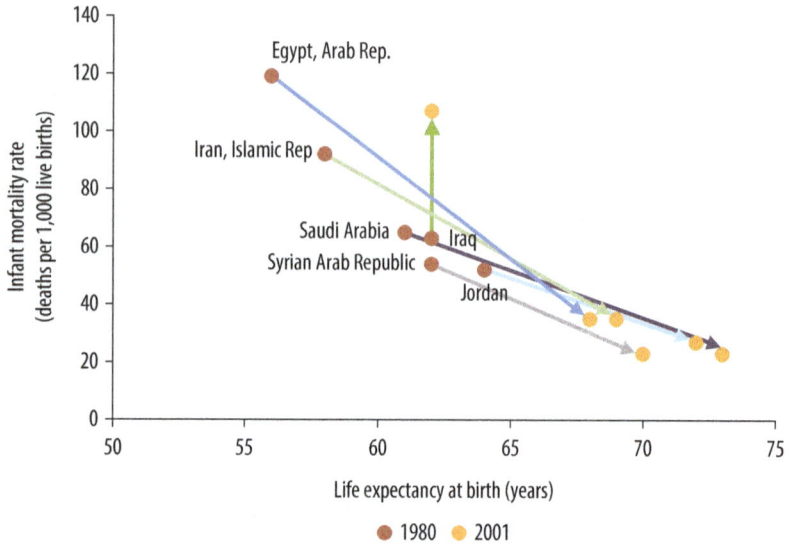

Source: World Development Indicators database (World Bank, various years).

From May 2003 to September 2012, the U.S. government spent around US$934 million on Iraqi health projects, both in construction and nonconstruction expenditures (SIGIR 2013). The Primary Healthcare Center project—its largest, at a cost of US$362 million—aimed to build 150 health clinics, but a review conducted by SIGIR found the program gravely deficient in its execution. The construction of the Basra Children's Hospital project was another flagship effort, but due to deteriorating security, poor site conditions, and poor contractor performance, basic construction took more than six years to complete. Other U.S. aid went to providing medical supplies and equipment for newly constructed or rehabilitated hospitals and clinics.

Many UN agencies also participated in health sector reconstruction, with UNICEF and the World Health Organization (WHO) the most active among them. UNICEF had retained a presence in Iraq since 1983 and began engaging in humanitarian assistance immediately following the invasion in 2003. WHO worked with the Ministry of Health to identify and address the most pressing short-term health needs of the population, while also strengthening health sector policy and systems by providing policy makers with valuable data on which to base decisions (Jones and others 2006). Many nongovernmental organizations (NGOs) also played important roles in supporting health or health-related sectors, such as water and sanitation. Although the activities of NGOs were undertaken based on grassroots needs, they were often fragmented and poorly coordinated. By March 2004, more than 85 NGOs were considered active within Iraq, but most of them had to give up a field presence due to the deteriorating security conditions.

Changes in Health Service Provision after 2003

The role played by the Ministry of Health was, as in other sectors, handicapped by capacity constraints. Per capita spending on health increased in the years after the invasion (figure 3.9). However, progress across many indicators has been modest. A major challenge to sector improvement has been the exodus of qualified health workers since 2003. According to some estimates, around 18,000 physicians—about half the national total before the invasion—have since fled Iraq. Of those who remained, the Iraqi government estimates that 628 physicians were murdered through 2011, although the Iraqi Medical Association puts the number closer to 2,000 (Webster 2011, 864). The death or departure of capable health workers and physicians has been exacerbated by the increasing influence of sectarian groups over the Ministry of Health.

After years of conflict, the number of people suffering from various types of mental health problems has grown significantly. A mental health survey undertaken jointly by the Iraq Ministry of Health, the Ministry of Health in the Kurdistan region, and WHO revealed high levels of

FIGURE 3.9

Health Expenditures per Capita in Iraq, 2003–14

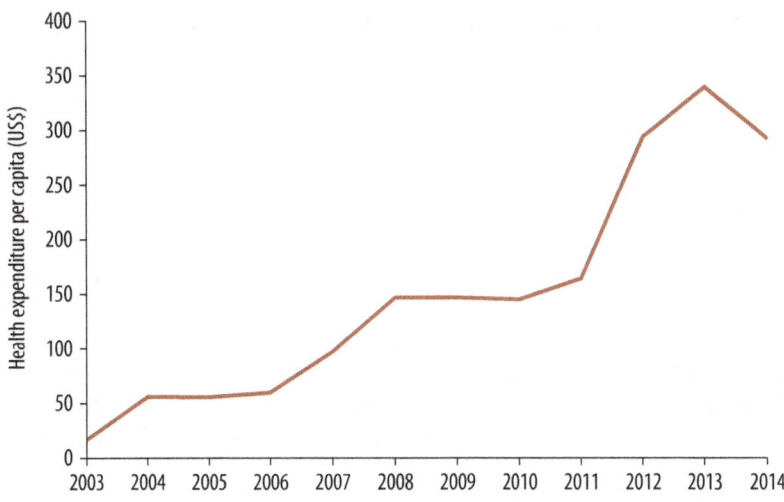

Source: World Development Indicators database (World Bank, various years).

FIGURE 3.10

Public Perceptions of Health Care Services in Iraq, by Region, 2011

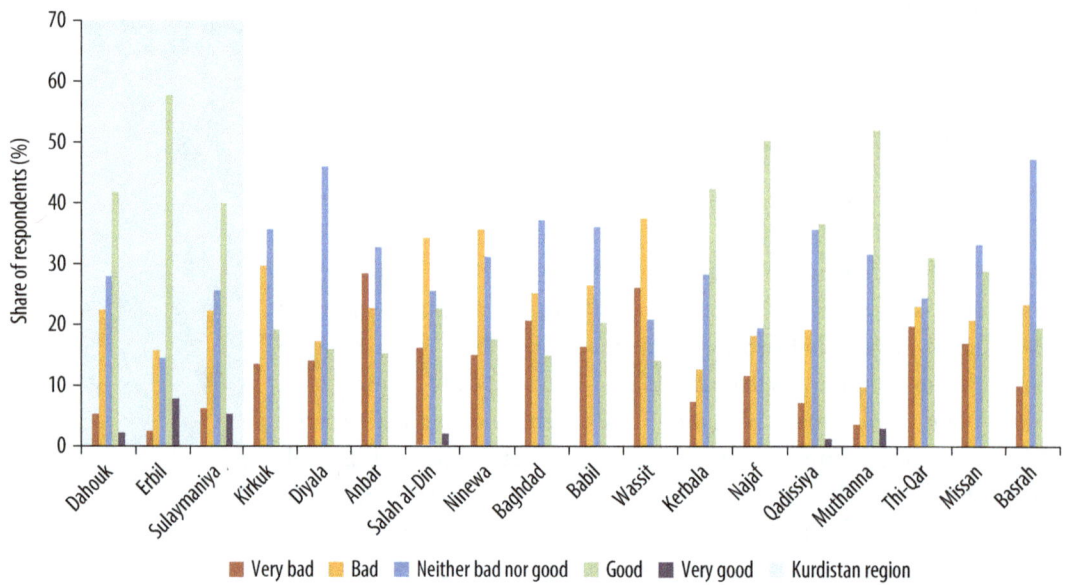

Source: CSO, KRSO, and World Bank 2011.

psychological distress in the population—finding, for example, that one in five women and one in seven men were likely to suffer a mental disorder in their lifetime.

As shown on figure 3.10, which captures polling data from 2011 on the perceived quality of health services across regions, the population in the Kurdistan region (Dahouk, Erbil, and Sulaymaniya) viewed the services they received more positively than the rest of the country. The Sunni-dominated governorates, as well as Baghdad, meanwhile, had a dim view of services in their area.

Notes

1. The electricity sector comprises several subsectors: generation, transmission, substations, and distribution. Although generating capacity was just one part of reconstruction activities undertaken in the sector, it is indicative of the sector's wider progress during this period.
2. The U.S. Department of State's Future of Iraq project conducted one of the few planning exercises for the electricity sector. And yet, even here, electricity was only tasked to one of the subcommittees of the Economy and Infrastructure Working Group, which, in turn, was one of 14 working groups under the project. Moreover, its recommendations were not incorporated into U.S. Department of Defense–led activities.

3. The United Kingdom offered to send oil experts, but U.S. officials declined the offer. Japan, for its part, provided concessional loans for efforts to rehabilitate major oil facilities, including the Basra Oil Export Terminal (US$500 million), the Basra Oil Refinery (US$445 million), and the Beiji Refinery (US$25 million). Norway also conducted capacity development programs.
4. SIGIR (2009) reports that there were nine fires.
5. USACE indicated that this figure could vary by as much as 40 percent.

References

CSO (Central Statistical Organization), KRSO (Kurdistan Region Statistics Organization), and United Nations. 2011. *Iraq—Household Socio-Economic Survey for 2011*. Baghdad: CSO, KRSO, and United Nations.

CSO (Central Statistical Organization), KRSO (Kurdistan Region Statistics Organization), and World Bank. 2007. *Iraq—Household Socio-Economic Survey for 2007*. Baghdad: CSO, KRSO, and World Bank.

———. 2011. *Iraq—Knowledge Network Survey for 2011*. Baghdad: CSO, KRSO, and World Bank.

IEA (International Energy Agency). 2012. *Iraq Energy Outlook*. Paris: OECD/IEA.

Jones, Seth G., Lee H. Hilborne, C. Ross Anthony, Lois M. Davis, Federico Girosi, Cheryl Benard, Rachel M. Swanger, Anita Datar Garten, and Anga R. Timilsina. 2006. *Securing Health: Lessons from Nation-Building Mission*. Santa Monica, CA: RAND Center for Domestic and International Health Security. https://www.rand.org/content/dam/rand/pubs/monographs/2006/RAND_MG321.pdf.

O'Hanlon, Michael E., and Joseph H. Campbell. 2007. *Iraq Index (September 2007) Tracking Variables of Reconstruction and Security in Post-Saddam Iraq*. Washington, DC: Brookings Institution. https://www.brookings.edu/wp-content/uploads/2016/07/index20070927.pdf.

———. 2008. *Iraq Index (March 2008): Tracking Variables of Reconstruction and Security in Post-Saddam Iraq*. Washington, DC: Brookings Institution. https://www.brookings.edu/wp-content/uploads/2016/07/index20080331.pdf.

PMAC (Prime Minister Advisory Commission). 2012. *Integrated National Energy Strategy: Final Report*. Private report. Baghdad: PMAC. http://documents.worldbank.org/curated/en/406941467995791680/Integrated-National-Energy-Strategy-INES-final-report.

SIGIR (Special Inspector General for Iraq Reconstruction). 2009. *Hard Lessons: The Iraq Reconstruction Experience*. Washington, DC: U.S. Government Printing Office.

———. 2013. *Learning from Iraq: A Final Report from the Special Inspector General for Iraq Reconstruction*. Washington, DC: SIGIR. https://www.globalsecurity.org/military/library/report/2013/sigir-learning-from-iraq.pdf.

Supervisory Committee for National Strategy for Education and Higher Education. 2012. *National Strategy for Education and Higher Education in Iraq*. Baghdad: Supervisory Committee for National Strategy for Education and Higher Education.

UN (United Nations) and World Bank. 2003. "International Reconstruction Fund Facility for Iraq, Terms of Reference." Unpublished document, World Bank, Washington, DC, December. http://siteresources.worldbank.org/IRFFI/Resources/RevisedTORS.pdf.

UNESCO (United Nations Educational, Scientific, and Cultural Organization). 2011. *UNESCO National Education Support Strategy Republic of Iraq 2010–2014*. Baghdad: UNESCO Iraq Office.

UNICEF (United Nations Children's Fund). 2014. *Country Report on Out of School Children*. Amman: UNICEF MENA Regional Office.

U.S. Energy Information Administration. 2016. "Country Analysis Brief: Iraq." http://www.iberglobal.com/files/2016/iraK_eia.pdf.

U.S. GAO (Government Accountability Office). 2005. *Rebuilding Iraq: Status of Funding and Reconstruction Efforts*. Report GAO-05-876. Washington, DC: GAO.

———. 2007. *Rebuilding Iraq: Integrated Strategic Plan Needed to Help Restore Iraq's Oil and Electricity Sectors*. Washington, DC: GAO.

Vogler, Gary. 2015. *Lessons Learned for the Energy Sector*. Kindle e-book. Fishers, IN: Howitzer Consulting LLC.

Waite, Jeffrey. 2003. *United Nations/World Bank Joint Needs Assessment: Education Sector*. Washington, DC: World Bank. http://documents.worldbank.org/curated/en/898741468262742934/United-Nations-World-Bank-joint-Iraq-needs-assessment-education-sector.

Webster, Paul C. 2011. "Iraq's Health System Yet to Heal from Ravages of War." *The Lancet* 378 (9794): 963–66.

Williams Lea Group. 2016. "The Report of the Iraq Inquiry—Section 10.01." Williams Lea Group on behalf of the Controller of Her Majesty's Stationery Office, London. http://webarchive.nationalarchives.gov.uk/20171123122743/http://www.iraqinquiry.org.uk/the-report/.

World Bank. 2011. *Confronting Poverty in Iraq*. Washington, DC: World Bank.

———. 2017a. *Iraq Public Expenditure Review*. Washington, DC: World Bank.

———. 2017b. *Iraq Systematic Country Diagnostic*. Washington, DC: World Bank.

———. Various years. World Bank Indicators database. Washington, DC: World Bank. https://data.worldbank.org/indicator/.

Yamao, Dai, and Keiko Sakai. 2013. *60 Chapters to Understand the Contemporary Iraq* [in Japanese]. Tokyo: Akashi Shobo.

CHAPTER 4

Institution Building, Governance Reform, and Private Sector Development

While most donors recognize the importance of institutional capacity and governance for implementing reconstruction and rebuilding the state, there is no consensus on how external actors can or should intervene to strengthen capacity. In Iraq, many donors placed higher priority on the recovery of economic and social infrastructure than on institution building and governance reform. This chapter assesses donor engagement in Iraq on capacity development, institution building, two key governance reform efforts—decentralization and anticorruption—and private sector development.

Capacity Development and Institution Building

U.S. Efforts to Strengthen Iraqi Capacity Development

Most donors focused on infrastructure recovery, but some also engaged with capacity development efforts to various degrees, with the United States playing the biggest part, at least financially. Early on, the capacity development activities of the Coalition Provisional Authority (CPA) were aimed mainly at rebuilding Iraqi security forces, with the rest of its focus placed squarely on infrastructure development. For example, when a US$18.4 billion supplementary budget appropriation was presented to the U.S. Congress, it consisted almost entirely of large infrastructure projects (Stephenson 2007). Still, U.S. capacity development efforts—led primarily by the U.S. Agency for International Development (USAID)—stand out financially among all donors. A significant number of USAID projects and programs included capacity development elements, with such efforts totaling US$4 billion. Unlike most of the newly created U.S. entities tasked with supervising and managing reconstruction activities, USAID was one of the few agencies with experience in postwar reconstruction. From the outset, it placed importance on institution building and governance reform. Aside from a US$2 billion contract with Bechtel to rebuild infrastructure, most of USAID's other activities related to capacity development and governance reforms (table 4.1).

TABLE 4.1

Major U.S. Agency for International Development Programs for the Economy and Governance in Iraq, 2003–12

Program and share of total	Amount (US$, millions)
Infrastructure (33%)	
Bechtel I	1,004.10
Bechtel II	1,180.00
Economy (16%)	
Economic Governance I	75.60
Economic Governance II	209.00
Agriculture Reconstruction and Development Program for Iraq (ARDI)	100.40
Agribusiness (Inma)	179.80
Harmonized Support for Agriculture Development	80.00
Private Sector Development (Izdihar)	140.20
Provincial Economic Growth (Tijara)	192.50
Financial Sector Development	51.20
Governance (51%)	
Health and Education	80.90
Primary Health Care Project	72.90
Revitalization of Iraqi Schools and Stabilization of Education I	55.30
Revitalization of Iraqi Schools and Stabilization of Education II	51.80
Local Governance Program I	224.40
Local Governance Program II	367.00
Local Governance Program III	207.60
Governance Strengthening	57.20
Community Action Program I	269.60
Community Action Program II	147.10
Community Action Program III	323.00
Electoral Technical Assistance	102.70
Elections Support Project	25.00
Voter Education	114.60
Community Stabilization Program	649.00
National Capacity Development (Tatweer)	339.40
Iraq Rapid Assistance Project	161.80
Administrative Support Project (Tarabot)	82.30
Total	6,544.40

Source: SIGIR 2013.

In interviews, Iraqi and former U.S. officials gave USAID's governance and capacity-building programs a mixed assessment. A common criticism was that, considering the amount of money spent on the programs, their outputs and outcomes were unclear. In particular, some interviewees felt that too much money, at least initially, was spent on consultant fees and not enough on expenditures that would have directly benefited the Iraqi people. But persons who attended USAID-sponsored training saw the programs more favorably. Since USAID's capacity development programs were ongoing, their methodology and content could be refined. Also, unlike other donors, USAID had program teams stationed in Iraq and was able to undertake many training activities within the country, which may have increased their impact.

Contractors and consultants played large roles in undertaking most U.S. capacity development activities, with U.S. reconstruction agencies such as the CPA and USAID awarding large-scale contracts sometimes exceeding US$100 million, most of which were conducted in-country. However, these contracts often lacked a predetermined goal and scope, close supervision, and effective coordination with other stakeholders (U.S. GAO 2007, 1–5).

Challenges in Evaluating Donor Engagement in Capacity Development Efforts

In addition to the United States, many other donors and international organizations were engaged in capacity development efforts: most United Nations (UN) projects funded by the International Reconstruction Fund Facility for Iraq (IRFFI) contained capacity development activities; the World Bank provided extensive training to familiarize Iraqi officials with World Bank procedures to enhance fiscal management capacity; the Japan International Cooperation Agency (JICA) offered various training opportunities to more than 6,000 Iraqis in neighboring countries, in the Kurdistan region, and in Iraq itself; and the U.K. Department for International Development and the European Union (EU) stressed capacity development while funding programs through the IRFFI.

These capacity development efforts have been subject to little evaluation, making it difficult to judge their effectiveness. This situation may not be unique to Iraq, however. The World Bank Institute points out that there is a lack of consensus among donors regarding what results should be expected from capacity development activities, and conventional monitoring and evaluation systems regularly fail to capture their impact (World Bank Institute 2012). One consequence of this ambiguity regarding impact was that international development actors provided a vast number of capacity development programs based on budget availability rather than the priorities of Iraqi institutions. Box 4.1, which details U.S. efforts to introduce a fiscal management information system (FMIS), provides a snapshot of some of the problems that this approach created.

BOX 4.1

Institution Building in Iraq: The Fiscal Management Information System

U.S. and World Bank efforts to introduce an FMIS in Iraq illustrate some of the challenges involved in delivering capacity development programs. USAID awarded contracts to a consulting firm under its Economic Governance I (US$79.6 million) and Economic Governance II (US$223.3 million) programs to improve public financial management. The centerpiece of these programs was the introduction of an FMIS, which aimed to connect public entities by a modern, automated computer system that would transfer fiscal and financial data and enable the Ministry of Finance to direct, monitor, and predict spending better. Despite the considerable resources spent on this effort, the system was never fully deployed.

According to research conducted by James Savage, four factors exacerbated the failure of the program. First, conflicts over management of the FMIS contract between USAID, the CPA, and the U.S. Department of Treasury's Office of Technical Assistance influenced the scope and administration of the program. For example, the Economic Governance contract called for the consulting firm to work closely with the finance and planning ministries, but the CPA restricted the access of USAID and the consulting firm to them. Second, the consulting firm chose overly sophisticated software programs without considering their applicability to the local context. Third, the prevailing security situation prevented the consulting firm from undertaking many activities and accessing the Ministry of Finance, which was located in one of the most dangerous areas of Baghdad. A contractor for the consulting firm was kidnapped by a militia in 2007, which halted most of the firm's activities in Iraq. Fourth, the program failed to obtain support and buy-in from Iraq Ministry of Finance leadership and other officials, who were comfortable with the existing system and resisted the introduction of the more sophisticated FMIS (Savage 2013).

After the Economic Governance II contract came to an end in 2009 without a completed FMIS, the task of introducing the FMIS was taken over by the World Bank under its technical assistance Public Finance Management Program (US$18 million). This component was added in the middle of project implementation, however, and internal reporting concluded that the World Bank program ultimately failed to introduce the FMIS.

We can learn several lessons from this case. First, a supply-driven approach without due consideration of the local context does not work. Second, donor mismanagement affects the outcome of programs. Third, avoiding past mistakes and transferring lessons between donors are difficult tasks.

Governance Reform: Decentralization and Local Governance

Since the fall of the Saddam Hussein regime, the devolution of centralized power—decentralization—has been a key and consistent governance priority for the postwar Iraqi government and the international community, just as it had been in the wake of collapsed authoritarian regimes elsewhere, such as in Indonesia after Suharto and in the Philippines following Ferdinando Marcos. The international community devoted substantial resources to decentralization efforts in postwar Iraq, particularly to developing the capacity of local institutions and establishing a new legal framework. A key milestone in this endeavor came when the new Constitution, which established federalism and decentralization as the guiding paradigms for the new Iraq, was ratified by a national referendum in October 2005. Nevertheless, as of 2019, progress toward full decentralization has been gradual and marked by little change of any significance.

U.S. Engagement on Decentralization and Local Governance

In post-Saddam Iraq, the United States was a strong proponent of a decentralized system, continuously supporting the policy agenda through a series of technical assistance programs. Even prior to the invasion in 2003, the promotion of decentralization featured prominently in U.S. prewar planning for what might follow the Saddam regime, with planners believing decentralization to be the best guarantor against the emergence of a dictatorship in the future (Kane, Hiltermann, and Alkadiri 2012). The expectation among planners was that by improving public services such as education, health, water, and roads through empowered, newly selected local councils, Iraq could be governed more effectively. Indeed, one plan called for channeling U.S. reconstruction funds through new local governments in order to break Iraq from the pattern of centralized authoritarianism that had gripped the country for decades, and local governance teams were sent into the country soon after the invasion (SIGIR 2009, 116).

USAID drove U.S. policy efforts to encourage decentralization in Iraq and provided assistance through a series of local governance programs. Table 4.2 shows USAID programs that contained elements of decentralization and national and local government capacity development. The United States originally intended to promote decentralization through both top-down efforts aimed at strengthening national and local governments and a bottom-up approach focused on enhancing civil society organizations. However, these efforts were, for the most part, ineffective.

TABLE 4.2

U.S. Agency for International Development Programs for National and Local Governance and Capacity Development in Iraq

Name of program	Program cost (US$, millions)	Operating period	Contractor	Program description
Local Governance Program I	224	2003–05	RTI International	To establish local councils and develop their capacity
Iraq Strengthening Local and Provincial Governance Program	367	2005–09	RTI International	To support Provincial Reconstruction Teams
Iraq Local Governance Program III	208	2009–10	RTI International	To support implementation of Law 21, 2008
Community Action Program	35	2003–05	Mercy Corps and four other nongovernmental organizations	To develop civil society and political participation
Tatweer	340	2006–10	Management System International	To develop capacity in central government and governorates
Tarabot	157	2011–14	Management System International	To improve public administrative capacity at the central and governorate levels
Taqadum	—	2011–14	Chemonics	To develop capacity in local government

Sources: Based on information from SIGIR 2013 and the USAID Office of Inspector General 2006, 2007, 2009.
Note: — = not available.

In addition, U.S. Ambassador Zalmay Khalilzad, who was posted to Baghdad in June 2005, shifted the focus of reconstruction efforts to smaller, local projects designed to provide jobs and improve service delivery (SIGIR 2013, 41). To promote this new policy, the Provincial Reconstruction Teams program brought together civilian and military personnel drawn from the United States–led coalition force and had them work as an integrated team. The initiative was tasked with building local government capacity and supporting projects for counterinsurgency and stability operations.

Initiatives by UN Agencies

Other donors, including UN agencies, also looked to support local governance. One such effort, the Local Area Development Program, was funded by the United Nations Development Group Iraq Trust Fund (UNDGITF) and involved the International Labour Organization; the United Nations Development Programme (UNDP); the United Nations Educational, Scientific, and Cultural Organization; the UN-Habitat; the United Nations Development Fund for Women; the United Nations Office for Project Services; and the World Health Organization. The program had three main objectives: (1) to strengthen the capabilities of local authorities in the north, center, and south of Iraq; (2) to stimulate local economic development; and (3) to improve social and physical infrastructure using a labor-intensive approach.

The Legal Framework for Decentralization

Soon after the invasion, efforts began to set up a legal framework for decentralization. The most notable achievement was the new Constitution, ratified in October 2005 by a national referendum, which defined a federal political system that included national and local governments. The drafting process started in May 2005, with the National Assembly's appointment of a 55-member drafting committee. Many political and sectarian groups held different views on many issues, but the question of how to define federalism and decentralization was among the most contentious. Proponents of federalism included the Kurdistan Regional Government (KRG) and the Islamic Supreme Council of Iraq (ISCI),[1] which managed to secure the inclusion of articles that limited the role of the central government and increased the role of regional governments. For example, article 115 specifies that all powers not stipulated as being within the exclusive purview of the federal government shall belong to the authorities of the regions and of governorates that are not organized in a region; with regard to other powers shared between the federal and regional governments, it stipulates that priority shall be given to the laws of the regions and governorates.

In 2008, a so-called "governorate powers law" transferred further powers to governorate councils (the Kurdish north is exempt under this legislation since the KRG is constitutionally recognized as a federal region). The law was amended in 2010 and 2013 to provide yet more authority to the governorates. Along with the 2005 Constitution, the law and its amendments provided a legal foundation for decentralization, addressing the overlap between the authority of local governments and the central government and granting broad legislative and regulatory powers to the subnational level. Despite this, attempts to devolve regulatory powers to regional governments were largely stymied by central government resistance to the move.[2]

Decentralization Stalled

Despite the wealth of donor-provided technical assistance and the steps taken to develop a legal framework, overall progress toward decentralization in Iraq after 2003 has been modest. The domestic political environment has been a key factor hampering progress, mainly the lack of commitment by political leaders and central government officials. Struggles over power, territory, and resources prevent political, religious, and sectarian groups from building a consensus on decentralization. Other challenges have arisen from disagreements over oil revenue–sharing arrangements; the role of the national, regional, and sectarian security forces; and disputes over the autonomy of the KRG (annex 4A). Experience in low- and middle-income countries suggests that successful decentralization always requires the right ingredients, appropriate timing, and some degree of experimentation. Donor support in Iraq failed to consider and address these elements sufficiently.

Governance Reform: Tackling Corruption

Widespread and intensifying corruption after the Iraq War hampered the reconstruction process and limited Iraqi public confidence and trust in the government. Although corruption was an issue in Iraq before the war, its nature and magnitude became far greater after the invasion. It is difficult to grasp the full dynamism of corruption, given its illicit nature. Still, the scale of corruption in Iraq remains among the worst in the world. In 2014, the Worldwide Governance Indicators ranked Iraq in the bottom 6 percent of countries for control of corruption (World Bank, various years). In 2015, Transparency International ranked Iraq 161 out of 167 countries in its global corruption perception index (Transparency International 2015). The nature and extent of corruption in Iraq have gone through several changes over the past two decades and can be loosely divided into three phases: monopolized corruption before the Gulf War in 1991, systematic and administrative corruption under economic sanctions, and an explosive rise in corruption after the Iraq War.

Corruption before and after 1991

Under the Saddam regime before the Gulf War in 1991, corruption was confined mainly to a small group of people in Saddam's inner circle. The Baath Party had a very stringent policy against corruption by public servants; corruption by civil servants—including ministers—was uncommon, in part because stealing from the state was considered stealing from Saddam Hussein and was punished accordingly. Harsh penalties were imposed on anyone who was even suspected of being involved in corruption, waste, or mismanagement (Al-Ali 2014, 192).

The Gulf War and ensuing economic sanctions changed the nature and extent of corruption entirely. Under economic sanctions and the Oil-for-Food Programme (OFFP), the practice of corruption became more institutionalized, with government officials demanding a percentage of kickbacks from contractors and suppliers. The Independent Inquiry Committee, otherwise known as the Volcker Committee, investigated corruption and fraud related to the OFFP and found that the Saddam regime earned US$1.8 billion in illicit income through surcharges on oil sales and kickbacks (Independent Inquiry Committee 2005). According to estimates by the U.S. Government Accountability Office, US$4.4 billion was effectively stolen through the OFFP, and an additional US$5.7 billion was lost as a result of oil smuggling. This was a systematic, illicit revenue scheme for the country, with the majority of benefits monopolized by a small group of high-ranking officials, the president, and his family.

Petty and administrative corruption within the civil service also became prevalent under the sanctions regime as public sector salaries declined (Le Billon 2005, 693). Iraqis had to pay for access to administrative, health, education, and judicial services. These practices had an impact on the collapse of state capacity and essential functions, and a large portion of the population lost access to key public services (Le Billon 2005, 693).

In the wake of the invasion in 2003 and subsequent turmoil, an even wider pool of the Iraqi workforce started to engage in corruption.[3] Many factors affected its spread: huge capital inflows, first from aid money and later from oil revenue; a breakdown in security and in the criminal justice system; and a weak legal and institutional framework that prevented an effective checks-and-balances system. Corruption took place in many areas and institutions and in different forms: oil smuggling, kickbacks from foreign and domestic contracts for public projects, administrative bribery, nepotism and clientelism, and political corruption.

The impact of widespread corruption was enormous in postwar Iraqi society. First, the Iraqi public's trust in public institutions, political parties, and the security and justice system plummeted. As a result, many people retreated into ethnosectarian groups or other institutions for service and security provision, which further degraded the authority of the state. Second, it impeded the progress of reconstruction activities in every aspect. This effect was most pronounced in the procurement process, as many parties tried to intervene in the selection of contractors by distorting the results of bid evaluations. This practice hobbled the functioning of public institutions, and although some public servants avoided these practices, their work was hindered by those engaged in misconduct and corruption. Third, corruption discouraged private sector engagement in Iraq, including foreign direct investment, since both domestic and international companies were subject to shakedowns in the course of doing business.

Foreign actors also played a role in exacerbating the state of corruption in Iraq. The International Advisory and Monitoring Board for Iraq and the U.S. Special Inspector General for Iraq Reconstruction (SIGIR) found a wide range of irregularities in spending out of the United States–managed Development Fund for Iraq (DFI).[4] These irregularities included a lack of competitive bidding for large contracts, missing contract information, payments for contracts that had not been supervised, and, in some cases, outright theft. An audit by the SIGIR, carried out in July 2010, discovered that US$8.7 billion of DFI funds was unaccounted for.

Anticorruption and Donor Assistance

After the invasion in 2003, the CPA established a basic institutional framework for anticorruption efforts in postwar Iraq. The CPA transferred supervisory authority from the Iraq Board of Supreme Audit to two newly created anticorruption entities. The Commission of Integrity (COI) was established by the CPA in early 2004 as an umbrella anticorruption entity in Iraq. Its functions ranged from investigating cases of corruption to developing a culture of integrity, transparency, and accountability in the public and private sectors. Offices of inspectors general, also established in 2004, were placed within each of the Iraqi ministries to provide independent internal oversight. Later, in 2007, the Joint Anti-Corruption Council was set up within the Prime Minister's Office to enhance executive coordination of anticorruption efforts.

The government of Iraq recognized the growing cost and impact of corruption on the country's economic development and reconstruction activities and, in March 2008, adopted the United Nations Convention against Corruption. In parallel, Iraq launched a national anticorruption campaign and in that same year rolled out a new anticorruption policy, the Baghdad Declaration on Combating Corruption. Based on these efforts, the first comprehensive National Anti-Corruption Strategy was developed in 2010 with support from UNDP and the United Nations Office on Drugs and Crime (UNODC). Based on an assessment of the country's concerns and vulnerability to corruption, the strategy included 200 action items to combat wrongdoing. The U.S. Embassy Anti-Corruption Coordination Office, UNDP, and UNODC engaged in several technical assistance programs to ensure implementation of the strategy. Further efforts and reforms were made to strengthen the legal framework and capacity of the institutions concerned.

Despite all this, corruption remains prevalent and continues to represent a critical challenge to effective governance in Iraq. The country's anticorruption initiatives faltered for several reasons. First, politicians manipulated investigations for political advantage, eroding the credibility of government anticorruption efforts (ICG 2011, 23–26). Second, oversight institutions suffered from institutional weaknesses from the outset; the mandates and job remits of both the COI and the inspectors general were unclear from the start. The COI lacked its own workforce to undertake investigations and so relied on the inspectors general for information, thus limiting its work to desk reviews. In addition, there was no clear process for hiring and dismissing inspectors, and they were subject to intervention by ministers, leading to the appointment of unqualified personnel selected on the basis of their relationship with the minister in question (ICG 2011, 10). A weak legal framework governing these oversight agencies continues to hinder their capacity.

Given the politicization of anticorruption efforts and the country's weak institutional and legal framework, the future of anticorruption reforms in Iraq remains uncertain. The required reforms identified through technical assistance programs and the country's current strategy are clear; the issue is whether sufficient political commitment can be mustered for the reforms to be implemented effectively. Without achieving tangible results, the Iraqi public's trust and confidence in the state will continue to suffer.

Private Sector Development

As far as the impact on the economy is concerned, the most critical shortcoming was that reconstruction made little progress in developing Iraq's non-oil private sector, failing to diversify the Iraqi economy away from its dependence on oil revenues. The high expectations for private investment in Iraq when military activities drew to a close in 2003 were realized only in the oil sector; in non-oil sectors, both foreign and domestic investment remained limited. This failure occurred even though many international donors prioritized development of the non-oil private sector. As a result, job creation in the non-oil private sector was nominal, and the public sector continued to be the primary source of employment in Iraq.

Donor engagement in private sector development focused mainly on the financial sector and the provision of microcredit, reform of state-owned enterprises (SOEs), and the promotion of private business, including through institutional and regulatory reforms. In this endeavor, the major actors were UN agencies, the United States, and the World Bank.

At the outset of the reconstruction process in 2003, the CPA led these efforts, setting three initial tasks to put free-market foundations in place: building financial market structures, promoting business, and determining the future of SOEs (SIGIR 2013, 114). However, the CPA's short-term mandate meant that it could make only a limited impact on the long-standing structures of the existing command economy driven by the state-run oil and natural gas sectors.

After the CPA passed from being, its initiatives were taken over by several U.S. agencies. Among them, USAID made several large-scale contributions, including the private sector development program known as "Izdihar" (translated as "prosperity" in Arabic) costing US$140 million and implemented between 2004 and 2008. Izdihar aimed to support the growth of micro, small, and medium enterprises by providing small grants and technical assistance. This program was followed by a provincial economic growth program called "Tijara" (meaning "trade" in Arabic), which cost US$192.5 million. Both programs included job creation provisions (SIGIR 2013, 116). Meanwhile, the Task Force for Business and Stability Operations, a division of the U.S. Department of Defense, was established in 2006 to promote foreign direct investment and reform of the SOEs. U.S. spending on Iraq's non-oil economy between 2003 and September 2012 was an estimated minimum of US$1.82 billion.

For its part, the World Bank undertook its own initiatives to stimulate private sector development in Iraq, albeit smaller in scope and financial scale. These efforts included conducting a business and investment climate survey, developing measures to encourage reform of SOEs and the banking and financial sectors, as well as providing support for public and private partnerships. Separately, agencies such as the International Labour Organization, UNDP, and the United Nations Industrial Development Organization also engaged in private sector development, including UNDP's formulation of the Private Sector Development Strategy (2014–30) on request by Iraq's Prime Minister's Advisory Commission. The strategy, produced in 2014, presented a road map for the Iraqi government and the private sector to promote private sector activities, but whether it will be fully implemented remains to be seen.

In the financial sector, a consensus priority targeted the reform and restructuring of the two large state-owned banks, Rasheed and Rafidain. Efforts to do so by the United States and the World Bank, however, ran into strong resistance. A more successful reform effort saw the establishment of the Trade Bank of Iraq in July 2003.

Supported by several foreign investment and commercial banks, the Trade Bank of Iraq was created specifically to facilitate exports and imports after the invasion. While it has experienced problems with management and corruption, its ability to facilitate exports and imports through the issuance of letters of credit was essential for many reconstruction activities.

Throughout the reconstruction of Iraq, the dire security situation represented the biggest hurdle preventing both foreign and local private sector actors from investing and expanding their business activities. The World Bank investment climate assessment in 2012, meanwhile, found that the leading constraints on private firms operating in Iraq were unreliable electricity supply, political instability, and corruption as well as public sector dominance and lagging education. The assessment also highlighted the need to reform market governance, invest in infrastructure and trade, strengthen factor markets, and reform the weak but pervasive SOEs as key priorities to enable private sector–led growth in Iraq.

Non-oil private companies are usually much more sensitive to risk factors than resource-related companies. An analysis shows that non-oil-related foreign direct investment, for which investors can choose areas that are subject to fewer risks, is negatively associated with conflict, while resource-related foreign direct investment is less affected by it (Witte and others 2016, 39–42). This tendency occurs mainly because the resource sector is more profitable, and resource companies are constrained by the geographic location of natural resources so that they are still likely to invest in areas experiencing conflict. And so it was in Iraq: even in 2009, when security was still very much in question, international oil companies were active participants in bidding for oil field access.

To promote non-oil sector development in Iraq, the international community needs to devise a better mechanism for reducing risk and a better financing facility. In February 2018, another international conference for the reconstruction of Iraq was held in Kuwait following the end of major fighting against Daesh. Hundreds of private companies participated in the conference. In its Reconstruction and Investment Framework, the Iraqi government and the international community emphasized the importance of the private sector in strengthening the country's economy.[5] As observed elsewhere in this study, the most critical shortcoming of the reconstruction of Iraq after 2003 was that it failed to develop the country's non-oil private sector. Stakeholders in reconstruction need to do better.

Annex 4A: Disputes over Decentralization in Iraq

The push for decentralization in Iraq has both supporters and detractors. The KRG and the ISCI support decentralization, seeing extensive devolution of power and the promotion of federalism as the best means to protect the interests and security of the communities they represent. Opposition to decentralization comes mainly from nationalists, Islamist Sunnis, and some Shia parties, including Dawa.

Disputes between each faction—those for decentralization and those against—center on three specific issues: oil revenue sharing; national, regional, and sectarian security forces; and the KRG.

Oil Revenue Sharing

The most contentious question raised by decentralization is how to deal with the ownership, management, and distribution of oil wealth. Iraq's oil resources are unequally spread geographically: about 75 percent of the country's oil reserves are concentrated in the south; about 17 percent in the north, including Kirkuk; and the rest in central western Iraq. Because of the disparity of oil reserves, oil wealth has become a major source of dispute across different regions, governorates, and groups. The 2005 Constitution defines a modality of oil revenue sharing in articles 111 and 112.[6] However, the articles provide room for differing interpretations, resulting in enduring disagreements between the KRG and the central government in Baghdad. The KRG has signed contracts with more than 25 oil companies and is now exporting oil and bypassing the State Organization for Marketing of Oil, an Iraqi national oil marketing company. This practice has met with strong opposition from the central government and eventually led the government to suspend fiscal transfers to the KRG. The ongoing dispute is closely related to a hydrocarbon law, which was drafted in 2007 and approved by the Council of Ministers, but which the National Assembly has yet to approve.

The National Military and Regional and Sectarian Security Forces

Another important issue that needs careful consideration in moving toward decentralization is how to streamline the roles of the national military, regional security forces such as Peshmerga, as well as religious and local militias. Ordinarily, national defense is considered a public good, typically provided by a national military force. In the case of Iraq, however, after the CPA's decision to disband the Iraqi military, security became a private or local good supplied to individuals by the group or groups—whether religious, regional, ethnic, or tribal—to which they belonged. For example, Sunni tribal security forces—the so-called "Sahwa" or "Sons of Iraq"—played a large role in fighting Al-Qaeda and bringing about a substantial improvement in the security situation after the U.S. military surge in 2007. Yet, after security improved, Sunni tribal forces were alienated by the Shia-led government, creating a security vacuum in the western central part of Iraq that was later filled by Daesh. As the fighting against Daesh in Mosul in 2016 shows, military forces in Iraq are composed of a mixture of a national military and Peshmerga and Shia militias. Incentivizing tribal and local security forces to contribute to the peace and stability of Iraq is a sensitive issue in designing the country's decentralization efforts.

The Kurdistan Regional Government

The KRG has been functioning as a de facto, autonomous regional government since 1991 and is a long-standing proponent of decentralization and federalism in Iraq. The KRG was first recognized officially in the Constitution of 1970 and was later given its own article in the 2005 Constitution, which entitled it to possess its own executive, legislative, and judicial branches and to govern its affairs autonomously within its regional borders.[7] Because of the suspension of fiscal transfers from the central government budget as a result of disputes over oil revenue sharing in the last two years, the KRG's autonomy has increased—but at the cost of a serious budget deficit. Resolving the KRG issue represents a central task in advancing Iraq's decentralization agenda. In the past, the ISCI had supported the formation of a large regional government encompassing southern governorates, an issue that has drawn much debate. The question of whether Iraq should allow an asymmetric form of decentralization or not, which would allow the KRG to hold a different status from the rest of Iraq, or whether Iraq should be split into three regional governments, needs careful handling.

Notes

1. The ISCI was forced to soften its stance on decentralization after its loss in consecutive elections in 2005 and 2010.
2. This tendency is noted throughout the literature. For example, see Katzman (2014).

3. In the final report of the U.S. Special Inspector General for Iraq Reconstruction, both Iraqi and U.S. officials expressed concern regarding this issue (SIGIR 2013).
4. United Nations Security Council Resolution 1483 called for the creation of an auditing body, the International Advisory and Monitoring Board for Iraq, to monitor DFI spending (UNSC 2013).
5. See http://www.cabinet.iq/uploads/Iraq%20Reconstruction/Iraq%20Recons%20&%20Inves.pdf.
6. Article 111 stipulates, "Oil and gas are owned by all the people of Iraq in all the regions and governorates." Article 112 stipulates the roles of the federal government, regional governments, and the producing governorates in managing and distributing oil and natural gas revenues.
7. Article 117 stipulates, "This Constitution, upon coming into force, shall recognize the region of Kurdistan, along with its existing authorities, as a federal region."

References

Al-Ali, Zaid. 2014. *The Struggle for Iraq's Future*. New Haven, CT: Yale University Press.

ICG (International Crisis Group). 2011. *Failing Oversight: Iraq's Unchecked Government*. Brussels: ICG.

Independent Inquiry Committee. 2005. *Manipulation of the Oil-for-Food Programme by the Iraqi Regime*. Independent Inquiry Committee into the UN Oil-for-Food Programme, October 27. http://www.foxnews.com/projects/pdf/final_off_report.pdf.

Iraq Ministry of Planning. 2018. *Iraq Reconstruction and Investment*. Baghdad: Ministry of Planning.

Kane, Sean, Joost R. Hiltermann, and Raad Alkadiri. 2012. "Iraq's Federalism Quandary." *The National Interest*, February 28. https://nationalinterest.org/article/iraqs-federalism-quandary-6512.

Katzman, Kenneth. 2014. *Iraq: Politics, Governance, and Human Rights*. Washington, DC: U.S. Congressional Research Service.

Le Billon, Philippe. 2005. "Corruption, Reconstruction, and Oil Governance in Iraq." *Third World Quarterly* 26 (4–5): 685–703.

Savage, James D. 2013. *Reconstructing Iraq's Budgetary Institutions*. Sterling, VA: Potomac Books.

SIGIR (Special Inspector General for Iraq Reconstruction). 2009. *Hard Lessons: The Iraq Reconstruction Experience*. Washington, DC: U.S. Government Printing Office.

———. 2013. *Learning from Iraq: A Final Report from the Special Inspector General for Iraq Reconstruction*. Washington, DC: SIGIR. https://www.globalsecurity.org/military/library/report/2013/sigir-learning-from-iraq.pdf.

Stephenson, James. 2007. *Losing the Golden Hour: An Inside View of Iraq's Reconstruction*. Washington, DC: Potomac Books.

Transparency International. 2015. *Corruption Perception Index 2015*. Berlin: Transparency International. https://www.transparency.org/cpi2015#results-table.

UNSC (United Nations Security Council). 2003. "United Nations Security Council Resolution (UNSCR) 1483." United Nations, New York, May. http://unscr.com/en/resolutions/doc/1483.

USAID (U.S. Agency for International Development) Office of Inspector General. 2006. *Audit of USAID/Iraq's Local Governance Program I & II Activities*. Baghdad: USAID.

———. 2007. *Audit of USAID/Iraq's Local Governance Program I & II Activities*. Baghdad: USAID.

———. 2009. *Audit of USAID/Iraq's Local Governance Program I & II Activities*. Baghdad: USAID.

U.S. GAO (Government Accountability Office). 2007. *Stabilizing and Rebuilding Iraq: U.S. Ministry Capacity Development Efforts Need an Overall Integrated Strategy to Guide Efforts and Manage Risk*. Washington, DC: GAO.

Witte, Caroline T., Martijn J. Burger, Elena Ianchovichina, and Enrico Pennings. 2016. "Dodging Bullets: The Heterogeneous Effect of Political Violence on Greenfield FDI." Policy Research Working Paper WPS 7914, World Bank Group, Washington, DC.

World Bank. 2012. *Iraq Investment Climate Assessment 2012*. Washington, DC: World Bank. http://documents.worldbank.org/curated/en/224621468261277147/pdf/770960ICA020120IRAC0Box377289B00PUBLIC0.pdf.

———. Various years. Worldwide Governance Indicators database. Washington, DC: World Bank. http://info.worldbank.org/governance/wgi/index.aspx#reports.

World Bank Institute. 2012. *Guide to Evaluating Capacity Development Results*. Washington, DC: World Bank.

CHAPTER 5

Lessons Learned from the Reconstruction of Iraq

Based on the analysis of international reconstruction efforts and the assessment of their impact on sectors, governance, and institutions, this chapter identifies lessons for international donors and organizations in the following seven areas: (1) working with institutions and cultivating national ownership; (2) effective implementation in insecure environments; (3) improving the effectiveness of donor funding for reconstruction; (4) enhancing accountability in reconstruction; (5) improving the assessment process and prioritization; (6) donor coordination with national institutions; and (7) procurement and contracting.

Working with National Institutions and Cultivating National Ownership

Interventions can weaken national institutions and social capital. While war often destroys institutions and social capital, poorly planned interventions by international actors can do more harm than good. The development industry often speaks of "doing no harm," but this analysis shows that the international community did significant harm to Iraqi institutions and society. The most devastating policy decisions—de-Baathification and dissolution of the Iraqi military—imposed significant constraints on government capacity. Similarly, the decision of the Coalition Provisional Authority (CPA) to form the Iraqi Governing Council along ethnosectarian lines only served to entrench distinctions between ethnic groups. Even seemingly minor actions can result in unintended consequences for national institutions, such as when better-paying international organizations draw qualified local staff away from public institutions. It is inevitable that external interventions will have a degree of influence over national institutions and society, for better or worse; however, international actors need to minimize the negative consequences as much as possible by considering factors such as history, ethnic and social background, the capacity of institutions, and the possible unintended consequences of their actions.

The drive for early results does not justify bypassing national institutions; donors should work through them. In a postconflict setting, international development actors often face pressure to deliver results quickly, making it tempting to bypass cumbersome systems and institutions. In the case of humanitarian assistance, the need to bypass national institutions can be compelling, but for medium- to long-term needs, cutting national institutions out of the process can cause lasting damage. Bypassing Iraqi institutions made initial gains less sustainable, as the reconstruction of Iraq's electricity sector shows, with power generation output declining in just the third year of operations due to a lack of Iraqi institutional capacity to operate and maintain facilities and equipment. The Special Inspector General for Iraq Reconstruction (SIGIR) concluded that physical infrastructure put in place by United States–funded reconstruction was already breaking down by 2005 (SIGIR 2013). This chain of failure was the product of a policy that emphasized rebuilding Iraq's physical infrastructure, but not the institutions to maintain it (SIGIR 2009, 258). Moreover, progress secured by external actors alone does little to build public confidence in the national institutions that are necessary for long-term stability. By failing to involve Iraqi institutions, international actors not only inadvertently weakened the institutions but likely also contributed to a loss of public confidence in them, creating room for divisive political interventions. In this sense, the international community missed opportunities to build an inclusive governance structure based on technical expertise.

Institution-building programs need to address local needs. Several factors specific to fragile and conflict-affected countries, over which donors had little influence, posed challenges for institution-building efforts in Iraq, including growing sectarian influence over ministry leadership and staff, pervasive corruption in Iraq ministries, and a distinct lack of security that limited in-country training initiatives. Still, donors created additional problems by failing to coordinate on what local needs were and how best to meet them, limiting the effectiveness of interventions to strengthen Iraqi institutional capacity. Solutions for more effective institution-building programs need to be based on a comprehensive review of the effectiveness of institution-building programs pursued in Iraq and other conflict-affected countries. One effective approach involves learning-by-doing through project implementation. Since international organizations can assess the needs and gaps within national institutions more accurately through the process of implementation, they can undertake more effective capacity development programs based on actual needs.

Systemic reforms need national political buy-in. During the occupation, U.S. officials attempted to impose drastic reforms with too little consideration of the local context, taking the successful interventions in postwar Germany and Japan as potential models for Iraq. For example, supporters of this approach equated de-Baathification with de-Nazification in postwar Germany, and believed that dissolving the Iraqi military would replicate the policy of demilitarization in postwar Japan. This perspective ignored the fact that Iraq's historical, social, and political background as well as its religious and ethnic heterogeneity differed markedly from those in Germany and Japan; as a result, the application of policies that sought to replicate these experiences had devastating consequences for Iraqi institutions. Similarly, steps toward decentralization could have proven more effective had U.S. officials not attempted to impose the policy from the beginning in a way that was perceived to be in concert with certain ethnosectarian groups to the exclusion of others. In fragile and conflict-affected states, as in any development engagement, donors and international organizations need to enhance national ownership of policies and gain local support before attempting to promote specific governance reforms.

Interventions can affect the behavior of national actors in unforeseen ways. Many interviewees for this research pointed out that the reluctance of Iraqi officials to make decisions became a major obstacle to effective project implementation. Factors such as intensifying political and sectarian divisions and fears of being subject to accusations of corruption often paralyzed decision-making processes. It is important to establish a functioning system to deter corruption; but if poorly implemented, such interventions can provoke unanticipated responses from national counterparts. This kind of unintended consequence is difficult to foresee, and measures that encourage positive behavioral change among national partners need to be identified.

Effective Implementation in Insecure Environments

Flexible implementation matters for effective reconstruction. While effective planning and preparation are important for understanding the local context and for shortening the lead-in time for reconstruction activities, without effective implementation, reconstruction efforts will bring few benefits to the recovering population. Effective implementation depends in large part on the ability to adapt and react to constantly changing conditions. In fluid conditions, implementation requires flexibility of thought and response. There are always gaps between the reality of needs and constraints on the ground and what reconstruction projects and programs are trying to achieve. Having insufficient and inaccurate information creates gaps, but implementation allows external actors to interact with diverse stakeholders and to understand the constraints and opportunities on the ground. Such knowledge is useful for reducing the gaps that existed at the beginning of projects and programs. In Iraq, the severity of the security situation was one of the key elements that reconstruction planners failed to anticipate. Donors and international organizations could have responded more flexibly by keeping a presence in the less volatile parts of the country, such as in the Kurdistan region and in some governorates in the south.

More needs to be done to improve remotely managed development operations. While remote management is always preferable to the outright suspension or cessation of aid and reconstruction operations, its effectiveness is nevertheless constrained. The delivery of aid is of lower quality and is less efficient, maintaining strategic programs is more difficult, and operations are more susceptible to corruption and often lack accountability. At the same time, while security risks are removed for outside personnel, they remain for in-country staff (Stoddard, Harmer, and Renouf 2010). In Iraq, international development actors had to devise creative approaches to manage project and program implementation remotely. To maintain interaction with Iraqi government institutions, many invited Iraqi officials to meet in neighboring countries or to connect via video conference facilities. They also used local staff and consultants, along with remote cameras and mobile phones. Still, an effective blueprint for remote development operations has remained elusive, and the full potential of new technology for remote operations has yet to be fully realized.

The importance of maintaining in-country operations cannot be overstated. While the Iraq experience demonstrated some of the ways in which development actors can continue to operate remotely, it cannot wholly replace in-country opportunities, which offer opportunities to interact with counterparts and enhance the effectiveness of assistance. The challenge for donors and international organizations is how to get the balance right between having a presence on the ground and avoiding unnecessary risks for employees. In Iraq, donors and international organizations could have responded more flexibly by keeping a presence in the less volatile parts of the country, such as in the Kurdistan region and in some governorates in the south where security was more stable, rather than opting for a near-wholesale withdrawal from the country when risk factors spiked.

Windows of opportunity can be crucial and fleeting. James Stephenson, a former U.S. Agency for International Development (USAID) country director, argues that the first year after the end of hostilities represents a "golden hour" in postconflict operations, when it is still possible to gain support from the public, something that occupation forces ultimately failed to do in Iraq during this period (Stephenson 2007, 36). The year 2003 was a dangerous one for international actors, as evidenced by the attack on the United Nations (UN) mission in Iraq; but in hindsight, it proved to be a great deal more stable than the years that followed it. In interviews for this research, several former staff members of international organizations questioned the wisdom of the decision to evacuate personnel from Iraq in 2003. Without staff on the ground, most donors were ill-equipped to react nimbly and, as a result, lost opportunities for effective delivery. If quick and flexible responses had been possible during this period, donor assistance might have contributed more effectively to achieving and consolidating stability.

Security and development go hand-in-hand. Development and security actors can succeed better by working together more closely early in the reconstruction process. In Iraq, development and security measures were undertaken independently and in a fragmented manner, a problem that endured for several years. Development actors were wary of being associated too closely with the occupation force, while the CPA and U.S. security actors had little interest in working with actors outside of the coalition. Only after the surge in 2007—by which time the U.S. development budget was being scaled back—did the U.S. military begin to reach out meaningfully to international reconstruction and development actors. This shift represented a growing understanding among security actors that without effective development results that provide economic opportunities and improve livelihoods, security cannot be achieved. At the same time, development actors recognize that without security, they cannot deliver on their priorities.

Improving the Effectiveness of Donor Funding for Reconstruction

Trust funds are more effective when operating in concert with national economies. Although the International Reconstruction Fund Facility for Iraq (IRFFI) played a role in reconstruction efforts, its impact on the Iraqi economy and reconstruction as a whole was limited. Donors, executing international organizations, and Iraqi institutions focused too much on the implementation of specific projects and programs funded by the IRFFI and not enough on their potential impact on the Iraqi economy and budget. With comparatively fewer available resources, operating in isolation limited IRFFI's impact when the trust fund mechanism could have encouraged beneficial multiplier effects for the Iraqi economy if it had been directed to seed broader investments from, and improvements in the effectiveness of, better-capitalized funding sources.

As it was, the link between interventions funded by the IRFFI and those financed by other sources, including the Iraqi budget, remained weak, even though donor funding could have had a role in reinforcing national budget execution. With regard to Iraq's capital investment budget, the availability of funds was less of a problem than how the money was spent, with a budget execution rate of just 40–60 percent of allocations (figure 5.1). If a donor funding mechanism had aligned resources with the Iraqi budget, the impact of assistance could have been greater. Instead, donors missed opportunities to enhance the efficiency of Iraq's budget execution. For example, working more closely with Iraqi institutions on management of the Development Fund for Iraq (DFI) could have introduced effective ways of spending the country's own resources, but the engagement of Iraqi officials was limited. Meanwhile, U.S. supervision of the DFI presented a poor example of

FIGURE 5.1

Budget Execution in Iraq, 2005–13

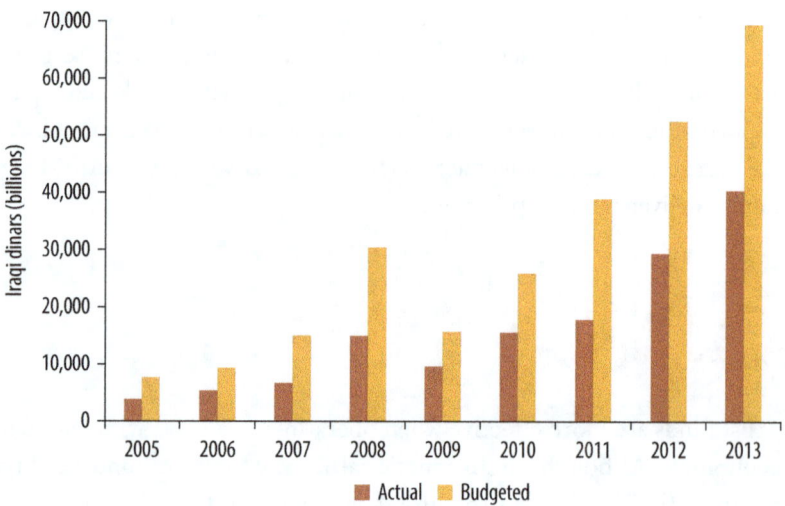

Source: Iraq Ministry of Finance, quoted in World Bank 2017.

budget management, subject as it was to fraud, waste, and abuse by the fund's managers (SIGIR 2013, 42). Loan assistance provided by the World Bank and the Japan International Cooperation Agency (JICA), which funded projects using a national execution modality that adhered to Iraqi rules and procedures, provided such opportunities to strengthen Iraqi budget practices, albeit involving relatively smaller sums. If an effective co-financing mechanism to pair loans with Iraqi budget expenditures had been implemented, both the impact of loan financing and Iraqi budget execution would have been enhanced.

Developing a sustainable, effective, and accountable budget execution system is essential to any reconstruction agenda. This was particularly true in the context of Iraq, which produced significant amounts of oil but paid insufficient attention to the importance of building an effective budget system. The availability of domestic revenues will differ from country to country; and for low-income, conflict-affected countries, external resources typically play a significant role in filling financial gaps. Still, even in these cases, donor funding should be used with a comprehensive view of the total resources available for reconstruction efforts.

Transparency in donor funding can improve national budgeting. Donor funding remained mostly off-budget, reflecting donor concerns that the Iraqi government lacked the necessary political and administrative capacity to allocate and use funds effectively and transparently (Savage 2013, 7). This meant, however, that actual project financing was largely opaque to Iraqi officials. The Iraq Ministry of Planning and Development Cooperation raised this issue in a report produced in 2007, pointing out that the off-budget financing of official development assistance prevented the adoption of a comprehensive national budget and that this made it impossible to achieve accurate and aligned financing processes that would complement capital expenditures (Iraq Ministry of Planning and Development Cooperation 2007). At a minimum, donors and partner countries should register reconstruction projects and programs with national budget teams.

Donor funding mechanisms can mobilize private resources. A donor funding mechanism, such as a trust fund, could have been used to mobilize resources from the private sector. Expectations for private investment in Iraq when military activities drew to a close in 2003 were realized only in the oil sector; in non-oil sectors, both foreign and domestic private investment remained limited. In fragile and conflict-affected settings, promoting private investment is difficult due to higher risks and the absence of legal frameworks, but without developing the private sector, particularly the non-oil sector, job creation and long-term economic growth in Iraq will likely be limited. The international community needs to find a more strategic way to leverage donor funding and use trust fund mechanisms to mobilize private investment, such as devising more effective mechanisms for lowering risk.

Enhancing Accountability in Reconstruction

Dual accountability can make delivering results on the ground more difficult. *World Development Report 2011: Conflict, Security, and Development* argues that donors and international organizations are accountable first to their domestic constituencies and shareholders and only second to the people of recipient states (figure 5.2; World Bank 2011, 26). This dilemma has consequences for reconstruction programs and can result in gaps between perceived needs and realities on the ground because international actors in-county are subject to strong influence from constituencies and policy makers at home, who may be less sensitive to the difficult, fast-changing dynamics of postconflict settings. In Iraq, the good intentions of international staff in the field often went unheeded by officials back in capitals.

Domestic pressures in donor countries also compel executing agencies to spend too much too soon. It is true that spending offers one way to measure progress; but in fragile and conflict settings, many projects invariably face delays relative to their original timelines. Similarly, a disbursement measure provides no indication of whether projects and programs are contributing to institutional development and achieving

FIGURE 5.2

The Dual Accountability Dilemma

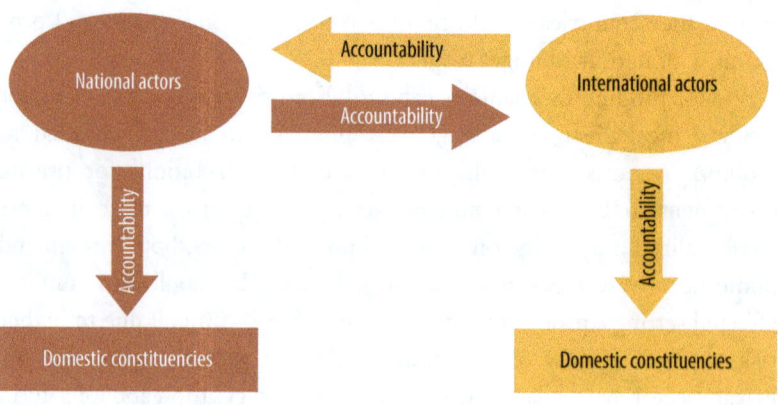

Source: World Bank 2011.

development objectives. In Iraq, faced with pressures to meet spending deadlines, many executing agencies opted to engage in simpler projects, the scope of which was limited to procurement and the delivery of materials and goods. In some cases, executing agencies were obliged to change the scope of projects in order to spend allocated funds within a certain time frame, regardless of needs on the ground. As a result, projects managed this way often provided limited benefit to their intended beneficiaries.[1] Every agency has its budget requirements, but meeting them without considering local needs can be counterproductive and wasteful and leave projects open to corruption.

The sources of reconstruction funding can affect domestic accountability. When financial resources for reconstruction come from external partners, they may not foster domestic accountability among citizens under less obligation to monitor spending. Since information on donor spending for Iraq's reconstruction was not disclosed to national institutions, citizens had no way to understand it fully. Domestically, meanwhile, citizens tend to scrutinize natural resource revenues less than tax revenues (Devarajan, Raballand, and Le 2011, 1–4). Thus, the use of donor financing and resource revenues for reconstruction activities has a limited impact on reinforcing domestic accountability between national institutions and citizens. In the case of Iraq's reconstruction, the fact that funding came primarily from external resources and oil revenues reduced the incentives for citizens to scrutinize spending, which might have affected the overall effectiveness of reconstruction efforts. Compounding matters, external resources as well as natural resource revenues became subject to interference from domestic actors seeking rents and private benefit.

Donors can exacerbate accountability challenges. Significant fraud, waste, and abuse were observed in reconstruction spending in Iraq. According to SIGIR, this situation was most commonly observed with the money disbursed from the DFI, and there were eventually several convictions related to fraud.[2] Still, waste was perhaps an even more serious problem. SIGIR estimates that US$8 billion of the US$18 billion DFI budget was wasted as a result of mismanagement. The fact that a donor had fueled accountability problems set a bad precedent for national institutions. In interviews for this research, many Iraqis pointed out that money distributed by military forces to tribal and ethnosectarian leaders in each governorate also fermented an environment that exacerbated corruption.

Effective monitoring mechanisms are needed. Monitoring the progress of projects and programs in fragile and conflict settings is another challenge to ensuring accountability in implementation, but an effective monitoring mechanism can be achieved by employing new technologies, engaging third parties, and involving multiple national actors. There are two interlinked approaches to monitoring: monitoring to ensure procedural and physical progress, and fiduciary monitoring to ensure transparency and accountability. For procedural and physical monitoring, many methods were tried in Iraq, but there remains room to improve the methodology by using technologies such as the Global Positioning System, mobile telephones, remote cameras, drones, and satellite imagery combined with a more effective use of local resources. For fiduciary monitoring, JICA and the World Bank each outsourced the task to third parties. While the World Bank employed a private company, JICA turned to the United Nations Development Programme (UNDP), exerting a constructive peer-pressure effect. UNDP assessed each executing agency's capacity and then provided capacity development programs based on the findings. This mechanism was strengthened by a quarterly monitoring meeting organized by the Japanese government and Iraq's Prime Minister's Advisory Commission (PMAC), in which the donor, executing agencies, and UNDP staff gathered to discuss implementation issues.

Improving the Assessment Process and Prioritization

The donor needs assessment process needs refinement. While the needs assessment proved useful for donors and the international community to understand the basic situation on the ground, the process could have been made more effective. For one thing, the UN's existing network in Iraq was not used in a systematic manner, and many teams began the assessment process from scratch. As a result, it took about four months to present the assessment results to the international community. While four months represented a reasonable time span for completion given the difficulties facing the assessment teams, drawing on the UN's existing networks and knowledge in Iraq could have shortened the process and allowed it to begin earlier, when security conditions were more stable.

The assessment placed more focus on physical damage than it did on institutional needs, with consideration of the latter limited to 14 sectors. This was perhaps inevitable, given the difficulty that teams faced in finding the right counterparts in Iraqi ministries. At the same time, however, there was a reluctance to rely on Iraq's national resources and networks since they had been part of the Saddam regime. While a country's needs and their relative urgency can change rapidly in conflict-affected regions, needs assessments tend to be carried out over only a limited period of time, typically very early in the postconflict period. In the case of Iraq, no systematic follow-up assessment was carried out, and the joint needs assessment became a one-off exercise. After that, identifying needs on the ground was left to each donor, with little coordination. The international community could have made the assessment ongoing and made the data available to a broad range of actors. Deteriorating security conditions would have made any follow-up assessment difficult, but employing remotely managed local networks could have sustained the process.

To assess needs effectively, an inclusive, whole-of-country approach is needed. In a postconflict environment, assessing the diverse needs of citizens is invariably difficult, but it is important for donors and executing agencies to diversify their network of national counterparts and information sources as well as their exposure to other parts of the country to foster an inclusive, "whole-of-country" approach. Even if an in-country presence is maintained, donors and executing agencies need to be mindful that being present does not necessarily lead to a better understanding of the country if their mobility is constrained and their interactions with national counterparts are limited. In Iraq, most donors based their operations in the highly fortified International Zone of Baghdad, and some rarely left it, restricting their interactions to those with colleagues and other international actors. At best, their contact with national authorities was limited to senior officials in the central government. But in a volatile political climate, a central government may not necessarily represent or fully understand the needs of the country as a whole, and perceptions developed through these limited interactions might be misleading.

Prioritization needs to be strategic. A lack of security and volatile political conditions constrained donor interactions with Iraqi counterparts and limited their ability to comprehend needs on the ground. As a result, projects and programs were selected for implementation opportunistically and based on incomplete information. In most cases, only limited reliable data were available to inform implementation decisions, and sector prioritization of infrastructure, human capital, and public services was rarely discussed. A supply-driven approach among donors also impinges on prioritization. From the outset of U.S. reconstruction activities in Iraq, there was a clear preference for "bricks and mortar" projects over those aimed at building human capital. The priorities of UN agencies tended to be driven by their respective mandates and areas of expertise. Of course, all sectors are necessary for the future development of Iraq; however, given the limitation of resources and absorptive capacity of national institutions, a more strategic approach could have been taken to identifying critical areas that required early engagement.

Assessments without follow-up limit impact. The lack of security in Iraq restricted what donors could do within the country. Thus, donors and international organizations have tended to engage in activities that can be undertaken without much of a field presence, such as analytical work, assessment of sectors and governance issues, and formulation of strategy. In the initial years after the invasion, U.S.-based consultants produced numerous reports on other countries' reconstruction experiences, since technical assistance contracts had been signed and they needed to produce deliverables to show that the money had been well spent. Yet, such analytical work was of limited value to Iraqi officials, who spent most of their time "firefighting" diverse problems on the ground and implementing projects and therefore had little time to review, let alone implement, the recommendations presented in consultant reports. As a result, many, if not most, of these publications—along with the financial resources that funded their production—have been underutilized since 2003. Donors and international organizations should avoid undertaking analytical work without first consulting domestic counterparts and actively engaging them in the process.

Donor Coordination with National Institutions

An effective coordination mechanism is a prerequisite for success in reconstruction, but it comes with costs. With most donors located outside of Iraq or confined to the International Zone of Baghdad, they spent a great deal of time meeting each other and focusing on interagency or interdonor coordination rather than visiting project sites or interacting with their Iraqi counterparts, who are so essential to implementation.

Coordination needs to have a clear objective. At the beginning, the mere exchange of information may be useful and encourage participation; but without substance and clear direction, it will lose momentum quickly and become unsustainable. To that end, there is evidence that the IRFFI served as a useful point of engagement between the international community and the Iraqi government, at least at the outset (Scanteam 2009). The cluster system established by the UN was less successful. While the cluster group played a large role in project and program selection for the United Nations Development Group Iraq Trust Fund (UNDGITF), it had little influence over implementation and results. At the same time, it increased the frequency of interagency meetings to an excessive level; cluster managers were sometimes selected without meeting any clear qualification criteria; and the participation of Iraqi representatives was only partially encouraged.

Better donor coordination can lessen the burden on national institutions. Too many projects in Iraq were undertaken with little coordination among donors and international organizations, causing significant confusion for the Iraqi authorities. The Donor Assistance

Database (DAD), which contains data covering 45 percent of total donor pledges, recorded that, in May 2007, 43 donors had pledged their support through some 16,931 grant projects with a total commitment of US$15 billion (some estimates suggest that these figures represented only 60 percent of total grant projects; Kanaya 2007). It is true that U.S. projects constituted the vast majority—16,435 out of 16,931 were U.S. funded—but excluding U.S. projects still leaves 496 projects, averaging US$6.4 million each. Since this figure captures less than half of total donor pledges, the actual number of projects was larger.

Practically, it was difficult for Iraqi institutions to deal with so many projects in light of their institutional constraints and lack of recent experience in dealing with donors; many donors chose simply to bypass Iraqi institutions rather than to help them better coordinate their activities. While IRFFI aimed to lessen transaction and operational costs and to enhance coordination among donors, its relatively small size limited its ultimate impact on coordination.

Aid effectiveness and harmonization have been critical development issues since the 1990s, and several related policies were adopted by members of the international community in the Rome Declaration on Harmonization (2003) and the Paris Declaration on Aid Effectiveness (2005). These policies encourage donors to enhance harmonization and coordination to improve aid effectiveness. The recommendations made in these declarations are of particular importance for operations in fragile and conflict settings, as the experience in Iraq demonstrates.

Better coordination can make capacity development programs more effective. In interviews conducted for this research, former Iraqi officials indicated the lack of coordination among donors and international organizations on the substance and approach of capacity development programs as a common problem. Efforts to support capacity development and institution building were diffuse and highly fragmented in both substance and approach. Iraqi officials claimed that this fragmentation led to serious confusion among Iraqi officials, who depended heavily on donors and contractors. Coordination was even lacking among U.S. reconstruction agencies such as the Department of Defense's Task Force on Business and Stability Operations, the Provincial Reconstruction Team, and USAID.

Procurement and Contracting

Procurement processes need to be flexible and harmonized. A flexible application of procurement rules and procedures is critical for implementing reconstruction projects swiftly and effectively. For most donors, procurement procedures were developed to operate in more stable environments; when applied in the absence of security, their stringent application will lead to emergency interventions being treated the same as those undertaken under normal circumstances, risking costly implementation delays. This mismatch in approach affected most of the donors engaged in the reconstruction of Iraq. For example, the CPA prioritized spending from the DFI and Iraqi oil revenues over its own appropriated reconstruction budget, because the DFI was not subject to U.S. procurement rules. This decision was understandable given the urgent needs on the ground, but it also raised the risk of financial misconduct in the use of funds. The procurement rules and guidelines of most donors should be revisited and adjusted to working in fragile settings.

Harmonization is another important effort for the donor community to consider. In Iraq, two approaches were taken to procurement: direct execution, whereby donors such as UN agencies and the United States directly procured contractors, goods, and equipment; and national execution, whereby Iraqi institutions were responsible for procurement, while donors such as JICA and the World Bank monitored the processes. In each approach, donors operated under rules and guidelines structured to secure the key procurement principles of economy, equity, transparency, and accountability.

National execution projects tended to take longer to complete than projects undertaken through the donor-led procurement process. In a weak institutional environment, procurement rules and procedures can be difficult to manage. As a result, those international organizations that adopted the national execution modality, such as JICA and the World Bank, found themselves in a situation where no disbursements were made on committed projects for the first several years. Considering the benefits and drawbacks of both direct and national execution mechanisms, one way to undertake procurement in conflict-affected countries is to employ a third party or procurement agent until a country has in place a better legal framework and more robust institutional capacity. In Afghanistan, the World Bank and the government adopted such an approach by employing a procurement agent. Under a hybrid model such as this, instead of starting a national procurement process from the beginning, for the first few years a third party, such as a UN agency or private firm, would be responsible for all procurement, operating with the participation of officials from counterpart institutions. Capacity development programs on procurement should be provided in parallel. Procurement responsibility can then be transferred to national institutions as capacity strengthens and legal frameworks are put in place. This mechanism would have positive effects on speed and also deter corruption.

Better contracting can reduce costs. Due to the prolonged violence in Iraq, all donors faced spiraling contract prices due as indirect costs, particularly those related to security. With U.S. contracts, in particular, such indirect costs often were incorporated into contracts, and direct expenditures on actual projects were disappointingly small. It is difficult to assess the precise percentage of direct and indirect expenditures since access to contractual information is limited, but research conducted by the Center for Strategic and International Studies estimated that direct costs might have been as low as 27 percent, with security consuming the lion's share of expenses (figure 5.3; CSIS 2004, 1). But the cost-plus, design-build contract modality adopted by U.S. planners also meant that contractors charged the U.S. government for all of their expenses, plus an additional amount for profit. In addition, limited contractual oversight led to several instances of overcharging, inappropriate sole-source contracting, inadequate reporting, and abuse (SIGIR 2013, x). Later, runaway costs associated with these contracts led to the introduction of fixed-cost contracts.

Another aspect to be considered is the relative size of contracts. In Iraq, contract management failures were experienced for large-value contracts in the electricity and oil sectors. When contracts were large, they were subject to more outside intervention and left many project

FIGURE 5.3

Estimated Breakdown of U.S. Reconstruction Contracts in Iraq

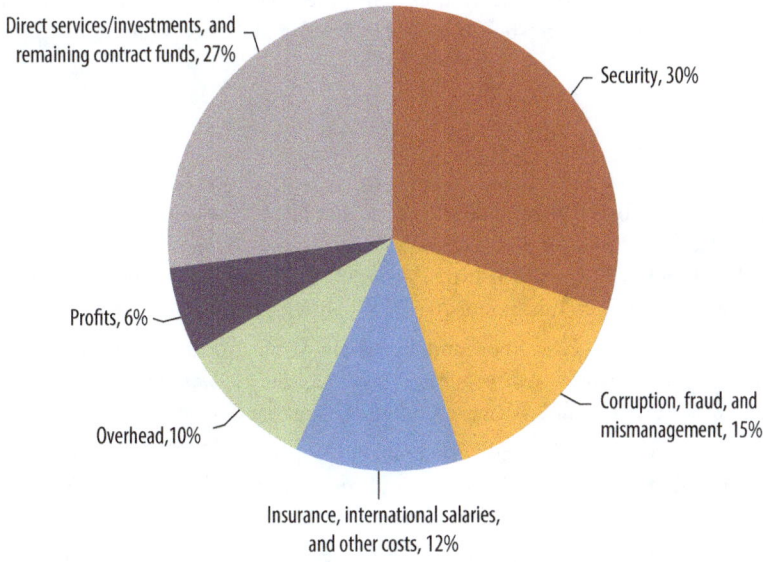

Source: CSIS 2004.

managers reluctant to make decisions for fear of accusations of fraud and corruption. This does not mean that smaller contracts are necessarily better, since bigger contracts can have a far bigger impact if implemented effectively; but donors should be mindful of the pitfalls of big contracts and manage the bidding and contracting process with extra care.

Rehabilitation projects do not always provide quick victories. Believing that rehabilitation, as opposed to new construction, was a quicker route to showing output, many donors opted for repair projects to avoid cumbersome safeguard processes, such as the preparation of environmental and social impact assessments, and the heightened scrutiny of new construction efforts. However, in practice, rehabilitation often proved more difficult than greenfield construction. Security challenges often made damage assessment and project implementation extremely difficult at existing sites. Meanwhile, many projects relied on contractors who were not involved in the original construction and who were less prepared for the challenges these facilities would pose. These factors made infrastructure rehabilitation projects in Iraq a bitter experience for key partners like Japan, the United States, and the World Bank.

Notes

1. For example, in an interview for this research, a former UN official described how Iraqi schoolchildren in some areas received multiple school bags from multiple donors, since the provision of school kits was easy to implement, even though the children were unable to attend school due to the prevailing security situation.
2. According to SIGIR (2013), among personnel engaged in U.S. reconstruction activities, 41 were arrested, 104 were indicted, and 82 were convicted.

References

CSIS (Center for Strategic and International Studies). 2004. *Estimated Breakdown of Funding Flows for Iraq's Reconstruction: How Are the Funds Being Spent?* Washington, DC: CSIS. https://csis-prod.s3.amazonaws.com/s3fs-public/legacy_files/files/attachments/041201_iraqfunds.pdf.

Devarajan, Shanta, Gaël Raballand, and Tuan Minh Le. 2011. *Increasing Public Expenditure Direct Redistribution, Taxation, and Accountability in Oil-Rich Economies: A Proposal.* Washington, DC: Center for Global Development.

Iraq Ministry of Planning and Development Cooperation. 2007. "Challenges and Lessons of Donors' Aid Management Process in Iraq." Presentation, Ministry of Planning and Development Cooperation, Baghdad.

Kanaya, Stepan. 2007. "Proliferation and Fragmentation of Donor Aid to Iraq." Report submitted to the Iraq Ministry of Planning, Baghdad.

Savage, James D. 2013. *Reconstructing Iraq's Budgetary Institutions*. Sterling, VA: Potomac Books.

Scanteam. 2009. *Stocktaking Review of the International Reconstruction Fund Facility for Iraq*. Oslo: Scanteam Analysts and Advisers.

SIGIR (Special Inspector General for Iraq Reconstruction). 2009. *Hard Lessons: The Iraq Reconstruction Experience*. Washington, DC: U.S. Government Printing Office.

———. 2013. *Learning from Iraq: A Final Report from the Special Inspector General for Iraq Reconstruction*. Washington, DC: SIGIR. https://www.globalsecurity.org/military/library/report/2013/sigir-learning-from-iraq.pdf.

Stephenson, James. 2007. *Losing the Golden Hour: An Inside View of Iraq's Reconstruction*. Washington, DC: Potomac Books.

Stoddard, Abby, Adele Harmer, and Jean S. Renouf. 2010. *Once Removed: Lessons and Challenges in Remote Management of Humanitarian Operations for Insecure Areas*. London: Humanitarian Outcomes. file:///C:/Users/O'Reilly/Downloads/remote_management_apr2010.pdf.

World Bank. 2011. *World Development Report 2011: Conflict, Security, and Development*. Washington, DC: World Bank.

———. 2017. *Iraq Public Expenditure Review*. Washington, DC: World Bank.

CHAPTER 6

Recommendations for Future Reconstruction Operations

Reconstruction in Fragile and Conflict Settings: Uncertain, Fluid, and Complex

Unlike the early post–World War II era, contemporary reconstruction operations are increasingly undertaken in volatile and insecure environments. Much of this has to do with the nature of conflicts today, which involve less interstate fighting and are more intrastate in nature, whether between states and nonstate actors or among nonstate actors. As a result, conflicts become protracted. Because reconstruction must be made to work in such volatile settings, we can find some analogies between the nature of war and that of reconstruction. Carl von Clausewitz described the countless factors that impinge on the conduct of war as friction (U.S. Marine Corps 1997, 5; von Clausewitz [1832] 1976). This idea of friction can be applied to reconstruction activities: friction can be external, such as the threats posed by terrorist organizations; friction can also be self-induced, caused by mismanagement of the donor process and a lack of coordination among stakeholders. Friction in reconstruction can result from uncertainty, fluidity, and complexity. While we try to minimize uncertainties by gathering information, we cannot eliminate them altogether. All actions in reconstruction will be based on incomplete, inaccurate, or even contradictory information. Meanwhile, policies that look good on paper may prove difficult to implement as a result of complex historical, cultural, societal, and organizational factors that are hard for external actors to comprehend.

Pursuing effective reconstruction within contexts of conflict and fragility is an exercise in minimizing these frictions while protecting vulnerable people and creating the conditions for lasting peace and stability. This study proposes four recommendations for the international community and external actors engaged in future reconstruction activities in conflict and fragile contexts.

Reinforcing National Success

Actions taken by the international community need to reinforce national success through national institutions. Imposing what the international community considered success, without due consideration of the local constraints and challenges or sufficient engagement from national institutions, failed in Iraq. Imposing external solutions invites counterproductive reactions from counterparts, no matter how effective such solutions may appear. In Iraq and elsewhere, successful reconstruction can only be achieved by rebuilding the national institutions and governance structures that provide citizens with justice, security, public services, and economic opportunities.

This approach is challenging. One of the biggest difficulties in working with national institutions in any future conflict-affected setting will be finding legitimate partners with which to deliver success, as we are witnessing in parts of the Middle East and North Africa—such as the Syrian Arab Republic and the Republic of Yemen today—as well as identifying national needs in an intensely divided political environment. In such a situation, a single entity—even a central government, if there is any—will not adequately represent the full range of needs of the country's diverse groups, and the government may well be constrained in what it can deliver in different regions. Since the political, social, security, and economic contexts of each country differ, there are no one-size-fits-all solutions. However, there are three key elements to engaging in reconstruction activities and rebuilding institutions within contexts of conflict and fragility: internal abilities, inclusiveness, and accountability.

First, donors and international organizations need to reinforce internal abilities within national institutions and avoid trying to replace existing capacity. The United States–led occupation authority, the Coalition Provisional Authority (CPA), initially tried to establish a parallel system for reconstruction by using its own experts and bringing in Iraqi exiles, which undermined the country's existing institutions and available human resources. Meanwhile, some international organizations, including United Nations (UN) agencies, adopted a direct execution modality that provided Iraqi institutions with only minimal roles in reconstruction. Bypassing national institutions may be justifiable in situations where the rapid provision of emergency humanitarian assistance is required to save lives. However, when it comes to medium- and longer-term recovery and reconstruction efforts, outcomes delivered by external actors alone will do little to reinforce confidence and trust among the people of a country and their national institutions. Weak national institutional capacity can certainly impede the progress of projects and programs in conflict-affected countries, but donors and international organizations need to remember that rebuilding a society's confidence and trust in national institutions is, in itself, an objective of reconstruction. Capable national human capital is likely still present in any postconflict situation. Undertaking reconstruction activities through national institutions can also provide an incentive for donors to focus on institution building instead of solely on individual projects and programs.

Second, the international community needs to reinforce inclusiveness in national institutions and help to cultivate the representation of diverse needs. There will always be constraints on communication in volatile states; and in a situation like Syria's today, reconstruction actors will also be faced with the conundrum of whether to engage with institutions that may have been complicit in committing atrocities. Working with diverse national stakeholders in an inclusive manner is not easy. However, adopting an exclusive approach risks alienating groups that—regardless of what they might have done or allowed to happen in the past—might be essential to successful reconstruction efforts. To foster an inclusive, whole-of-country approach, donors and international organizations would be well served by diversifying their network of national counterparts and information sources, as well as increasing their exposure to different parts of the country. The role of the international community is to facilitate the creation of an inclusive mechanism that reflects diverse needs and engages diverse stakeholders. In this regard, decentralization can be one approach, but as post-2003 efforts in Iraq show, promoting decentralization is far from easy. Whether decentralization contributes to achieving peace and stability depends on the design and sequence of actions embedded in its introduction. The key is to find a governance mechanism that ensures inclusiveness.

Third, external actors in international reconstruction should reinforce accountability in the relationship between national institutions and citizens. *World Development Report 2004: Making Services Work for Poor People* argues that foreign donors should reinforce accountability in the relationships among key stakeholders in service delivery (World Bank 2004, 10). Fostering accountability is also a key challenge for international reconstruction efforts in fragile contexts. When financial resources for reconstruction come from external partners, however, they may not foster domestic accountability, because citizens feel less of an obligation to monitor spending for which they have not paid. Similarly, citizens tend to scrutinize natural resource revenues less than revenues derived from public sources, such as taxes. For these reasons, using donor financing and resource revenues for reconstruction activities often does little to reinforce accountability in national institutions.

One proposal to enhance accountability as well as the effectiveness of reconstruction funding is to revisit the mechanism for distributing resources. Devarajan and colleagues argue that, by transferring a portion of natural resource–related government revenues uniformly and universally as direct payments to the population, some countries could increase both private consumption and the provision of public goods and thereby reduce poverty and enhance social welfare (Devarajan and others 2013, 7). The total financial commitment for the reconstruction of Iraq amounted to US$220.1 billion—somewhere between US$7,000 and US$9,000 per capita—much of which is thought to have been ineffective in improving the lives of Iraqis, making this proposal worth considering in the context of reconstruction funding.

Balancing Time and Scale in Operations

International and domestic actors need to strike the right balance between seeking smaller, short-term victories and pursuing interventions that result in larger, longer-term gains. The magnitude of ineffectiveness and waste in spending during reconstruction in Iraq, coupled with tightening resources, can lead international actors to conclude that smaller-scale interventions are the best way to engage in reconstruction. While true that smaller-scale approaches minimize risks, the impact of intervention will be invariably smaller even while the management and administrative costs for each intervention may stay the same, rendering such interventions proportionately more expensive. Seizing windows of opportunity through quick engagement is important for engaging in effective reconstruction and restoring confidence among the public, but an excessive focus on short-term wins can compromise long-term, sustainable gains—as early efforts in Iraq's electricity sector demonstrate.

Large-scale, flagship-type projects, if implemented successfully, can help to build public support for reconstruction efforts. In interviews for this research, some Iraqi officials pointed out that few of Iraq's reconstruction funds went toward symbolic, legacy projects, which made it difficult for Iraqis to see tangible signs of what reconstruction efforts were achieving. Despite their importance as a means of galvanizing popular support for reconstruction, however, larger-scale projects tend to take longer to complete and can be subject to interference from rent seekers, among others.

One effective approach is to begin with small-scale, short-term interventions that can be scaled up later if the initial engagement is successful. Reconstruction actors and policy makers need to prepare well-structured project portfolios that balance time and scale in operations. Finding the right balance between short- and long-term projects depends on two elements: first, whether the approach will help to build public confidence in national institutions; and, second, whether it will drive positive behavioral change among the public and government officials. *World Development Report 2011: Conflict, Security, and Development* argues that quick victories might help to restore confidence in the government's ability to deal with violent threats, whereas the implementation of institutional and social changes takes time. Early results might enhance the morale of national institutions, driving positive behavioral change and setting the right incentives for long-term institution building (World Bank 2011, 13). Intangible elements—such as confidence, incentives, and morale—matter when striving for the right balance between time and scale.

Promoting Private Sector Engagement in Fragile Settings

The international community needs to find a better mechanism to support private sector activities in fragile settings. Without strong private sector engagement, a lasting recovery cannot be achieved. In Iraq, the most critical shortcoming was that reconstruction failed to diversify the Iraqi economy away from the dominant oil sector; as a result, few economic opportunities were created in the non-oil private sector.

The biggest hurdle to private sector development in Iraq was the dire security situation, which discouraged both foreign and local private actors from investing and expanding their business activities. A separate analysis has shown that non-resource-related foreign direct investment is negatively associated with conflict, while resource-related foreign direct investment is less affected (Witte and others 2016, 39–42). This finding is consistent with the experience in Iraq, where international oil companies were active in bidding for access even when security was lacking, while investment in non-oil sectors was limited in all areas but the relatively safer Kurdistan region. Elsewhere in the country, the role of the private sector was confined mostly to that of contractor for donor- and government-funded projects. The international community can play a part in finding a better mechanism for lowering the risks for private actors.

Reinforcing the Security-Development Nexus

The international community needs to integrate the work of the security and development spheres. Security and reconstruction actors failed to effectively coordinate their efforts in Iraq for several reasons. First, there have been historical difficulties in connecting security and development actors in reconstruction, and Iraq was no exception. Coalition forces played a significant role in reconstruction, but the lines of authority and command between development and security actors in early U.S. reconstruction efforts lacked clarity, creating tensions and confusion among the different parties. To address the divide between development and security actors, the United States created integrated civil-military coordination units in the Provincial Reconstruction Teams. Meanwhile, unlike those programs conducted by development organizations, security forces–led reconstruction activities had no established evaluation process.

Second, security risks can only be fully neutralized by addressing the root causes of violence and extremism through a development approach that contributes to providing economic opportunities, especially among young people. The 2017 Arab Youth Survey raised possible links between unemployment and the potential for radicalization, with young Arabs perceiving unemployment and extremism as the biggest problems holding back the Middle East and North Africa region (ASDA'A Burson-Marsteller 2017, 20–23). Approximately a quarter of those surveyed said that they consider education reform and employment generation as key to defeating terrorism. In Iraq, because of the high concentration of resources in the oil sector, other sectors have developed little and created few job opportunities. Economic diversification and job creation can address the root causes of violence and extremism. Successful reconstruction depends on whether the members of society who feel excluded today are given opportunities and reasons for hope.

Developing and strengthening inclusive partnerships between the security and development spheres is of paramount importance for success in reconstruction. It is time for the international community to devise a new mechanism for coordinating the responses to security and development challenges.

The Future of Reconstruction in Fragile and Conflict Settings

Pursuing effective reconstruction within contexts of conflict and fragility is extremely difficult; it requires a deep understanding of the challenges and a delicate touch. The international community is still learning how to support effective and durable postconflict reconstruction; its failure to do so in Iraq has had severe consequences for the region and the world. Successful reconstruction efforts require external actors to understand national and local contexts, to build effective relationships with diverse national and local actors, and to manage these relationships and expectations in contexts of extreme danger and volatility. External actors also need to respond to and navigate their own priorities and objectives, even if these priorities contradict local needs and contexts. Amid such intense and complex difficulties, the international community may hesitate to engage in robust reconstruction activities, but the cost of inaction is also significant. The success or failure of country-level reconstruction efforts can have a significant impact on the peace and stability of the broader global community. To improve outcomes in the future, international actors need to understand the weight of their responsibility and take the actions necessary to learn from past mistakes.

References

ASDA'A Burson-Marsteller. 2017. *Arab Youth Survey 2017: The Middle East–Region Divided.* White Paper. Dubai Media City: ASDA'A Burson Marsteller. https://www.arabyouthsurvey.com/pdf/whitepaper/en/2017-AYS-White-Paper.pdf.

Devarajan, Shantayanan, Marcelo M. Giugale, Helene Ehrhart, Tuan Minh Le, and Huong Nguyen. 2013. *The Case for Direct Transfers of Resource Revenues in Africa.* Washington, DC: Center for Global Development.

U.S. Marine Corps. 1997. *Warfighting.* Washington, DC: U.S. Government Printing Office. https://www.marines.mil/Portals/59/Publications/MCDP%201%20Warfighting.pdf.

von Clausewitz, Carl. (1832) 1976. *On War,* trans. Michael Howard and Peter Paret. Princeton, NJ: Princeton University Press.

Witte, Caroline T., Martijn J. Burger, Elena Ianchovichina, and Enrico Pennings. 2016. "Dodging Bullets: The Heterogeneous Effect of Political Violence on Greenfield FDI." Policy Research Working Paper WPS 7914, World Bank Group, Washington, DC.

World Bank. 2004. *World Development Report 2004: Making Services Work for Poor People.* Washington, DC: World Bank.

———. 2011. *World Development Report 2011: Conflict, Security, and Development.* Washington, DC: World Bank.

www.ingramcontent.com/pod-product-compliance
Lightning Source LLC
Chambersburg PA
CBHW082212300426
44117CB00016B/2770